AQA Drama

GCSE

Pauline Courtice

Susan Elles

Rob Thomson

Series editor

Susan Elles

Published in 2009 by:
Nelson Thornes Ltd
Delta Place
27 Bath Road
CHELTENHAM
GL53 7TH
United Kingdom

13 14 15 16 / 10 9 8 7 6 5 4 3 2

A catalogue record for this book is available from the British Library

ISBN 978 1 4085 0410 9

Cover photograph/illustration: Alamy/ Nir Alon
Page make-up by Pantek Arts Ltd

Printed and bound in Spain by GraphyCems

The authors and publisher are grateful to the following for permission to reproduce the following copyright material:

Photograph acknowledgements: Chapter 1 opener and 1A © Getty Images; 1B, 1.2A reproduced by permission of Chris Radcliffe; 1.1A © Newsquest Media Group Ltd; Chapter 2 opener © Rex Features/Donald Cooper; 2A reproduced by permission of The Point, Eastleigh; 2.1A reproduced by kind permission of Sally Marchant ; 2.1B © ArenaPAL/Robert Day; 2.2A © Mike Eddowes; 2.2B Performance shot – from NIE's show – *The End of Everything Ever*; 2.4A © Mike Abrahams/Alamy; 2.4B, 5.7A, 5.7B courtesy of Helen Cadbury/Pilot Theatre; 2.5A, 2.9A, 4.4B, 4.14A, 5A, 5.3A, 7.2A, 7.2B, 7.3A, 7.3B, 7.3D, 7.4A reproduced courtesy of Orange Tree Theatre, Richmond. Photographer: Robert Day. With thanks to Katie Henry; 2.5B reproduced by kind permission of Forest Arts Centre, Company Gavin Robertson, actors (left to right) Wayne Forester and Gavin Robertson and photographer Ian Parsons; 2.6A © Keith Morris/Alamy; 2.6B performance shot – from NIE's show – *The End of Everything Ever*; 2.7A, 2.7B, 4.4A, 4.5A 610B © Colin Willoughby/ArenaPAL; 2.8A reproduced by permission of Lightversus; 2.10A, 2.11A, 3.7A reproduced by permission of HumDrum Theatre Company, Portsmouth; 2.12A, page 39A, Chapter 4 opener © Rex Features/Alastair Muir; 2.13A photograph from *Water* by Filter Theatre at the Lyric Hammersmith, 2007. Reproduced by kind permission of photographer, Edward Dimsdale; 2.14A, 7.2C © to be deleted/Alamy; Chapter 3 opener, 3.2E, 3.3A, 3.4A, 3.11B, © Malcolm Davies Collection, The Shakespeare Birthplace Trust/ArenaPAL; 3A © ArenaPAL; 3B © Alamy/Joe Devenney; 3.1A reproduced by permission of HumDrum Theatre Company, photographer: Roger Taylor; 3.1B, Chapter 6 opener © Getty Images/AFP; 3.2A © Achim Prill/iStockphoto; 3.2B © EPO Online; 3.2H © Suzanne Worthington/Royal Shakespeare Company/ArenaPAL; 3.4B © Getty Images; 3.4C, 3.5B © Moviestore Collection; 3.5A © Getty Images; 3.6A, 3.10A © Pete Jones/ArenaPAL; 3.7B, 5.3B, 5.11A reproduced by kind permission of Bishop's College, Gloucester, with thanks to Barnaby Eaton-Jones and pupils; 3.8A © Horse and Bamboo Theatre/Ian Tilton; 3.11A © Clive Barda/ArenaPAL; 4A © Marilyn Kingwall/ArenaPAL; 4.1A © David Sacks/Getty Images; 4.1B, 4.2A, 4.14C, 4.3B courtesy of The Nuffield Theatre 2007, photograph by Mike Eddowes; 4.3A © Content Mine International/Alamy; 4.6A © Sheila Burnett/ArenaPAL; 4.7A © John Timbers/ArenaPAL; 4.8A © Mat Hayward/Fotolia; 4.9A reproduced by permission of Pauline Courtice; 4.10A © Tristram Kenton/Lebrecht Music & Arts; 4.11A © Bodleian Library, University of Edinburgh, shelfmark: MS. Bodl. 264, fol. 54v; Chapter 5 opener © Alamy/Powys Photo; 5.1A, 5.2A, 5.4A, 5.5A © Dom Beardmore/ArenaPAL; 5.1B © Nigel R. Barklie/Rex Features; 5.6A reproduced by permission from the production The Shadow Box at the University of Derby, photograph by Matt Howcroft; 5.8A reproduced by kind permission of Rhubarb Theatre, photographer: Phil Crow; 5.8B reproduced by permission of HumDrum Theatre Company, Portsmouth, photographer Russell Blitz; 5.10A, 7.3C reproduced by kind permission of HumDrum Theatre Company, Portsmouth, photographer Stephen Rose; 5.9A © iStockphoto; 5.10B © Image Theatre, Prague; 5.12A © Mike Goldwater/Alamy; 6.1A © ArenaPAL; 6.1B © Bernie Epstein/Alamy; 6.1C © Getty Images; 6.1D © Holmes Garden Photos/Alamy; 6.2A © Eddie Webb/ArenaPAL; 6.2B © Eddie Mulholland/Rex Features; 6.2C © Uppa/Topfoto; 6.2C © Norbert Schaefer/Corbis; 6.2E © Rowan Tolley/ArenaPAL; 6.2F © ArenaPAL; 6.3C © Swim Ink 2 LLC/Corbis; 6.3E © Johnny Greig/Alamy; 6.4A © Royal Exchange Theatre Manchester; 6.6A © Imagebroker/Alamy; 6.7A © Richard Mildenhall/ArenaPAL; 6.8A © Mary Evans Picture Library; 6.8B © Garry Gay/Getty Images; 6.9A © Sheila Burnett/ArenaPAL; 6.11A © iStockphoto; 6.12A © Alamy INTERFOTO Pressebildagentur; Chapter 7 opener © Getty Images; 7.4C reproduced by kind permission of the King's Theatre, Southsea.

Text acknowledgements: 2.3 *The Theban Plays* by Sophocles, translated with an introduction by E.F. Watling (Penguin Classics, 1947). Copyright © E.F. Watling, 1947. Reproduced by permission of Penguin Books Ltd; *Metamorphosis* by Franz Kafka, published by Vintage. Reprinted by permission of The Random House Group Ltd; 2.4 Benjamin Zephaniah, *City Psalms* (Bloodaxe Books, 1992); 4.3 Edited *Twelfth Night* extract courtesy of Steve Gooch, creator of 'The Cut Shakespeare' series of Shakespeare texts edited for performance and reading aloud is the author of four dozen works for the stage including *Female Transport*, performed some 500 times around the world, and *Writing a Play*, based on his popular playwriting class. 'A Memory of Lizzie' taken from *Sepia and Song* (Drama Anthologies) by David Foxton (Nelson Thornes 2000).

Every effort has been made to contact the copyright holders and we apologise if any have been overlooked. Should copyright have been unwittingly infringed in this book, the owners should contact the publishers, who will make corrections at reprint.

Contents

Nelson Thornes has worked hard to ensure this book and the accompanying online resources offer you excellent support for your GCSE course. You can be sure that it gives you useful support throughout your course.

These print and online resources together **unlock blended learning**; this means that the links between the assessment questions in the book and the revision activities online blend together to maximise your understanding of a topic and help you achieve your potential.

These online resources are available on  kerboodle which can be accessed via the internet at **www.kerboodle.com/live**, anytime, anywhere. If your school or college subscribes to kerboodle you will be provided with your own personal login details. Once logged in, access your course and locate the required activity.

For more information and help on how to use kerboodle visit **www.kerboodle.com**

How to use this book

Objectives

Look for the list of **Learning Objectives** based on the requirements of this course so you can ensure you are covering the key points required.

Study tip

Don't forget to read the **Study Tips** throughout the book as well as answering **Practice Questions**.

Visit **www.nelsonthornes.com** for more information.

Practice questions are reproduced by permission of the Assessment and Qualifications Alliance.

Welcome to GCSE Drama

Welcome! Drama is an exciting subject. Now you have opened this book, come and see what we have to offer. All that is needed is a bit of interest and a willingness to have a go. Everything else will come to you as you work your way through the course.

Why choose Drama?

Drama is a practical subject. It deals with people. Drama involves looking at people's thoughts, their feelings and their relationships with each other and with the world about them. Through Drama we can see into the lives of others and perhaps even make sense of our own.

For thousands of years people have made audiences laugh or cry by acting out stories that were important to them. Even today audiences can feel sympathy with characters created by the ancient Greeks or join in the laughter and songs of traditional English **mummers'** or **pace-egg plays**. By doing GCSE Drama you can become part of those traditions and learn how to present stories and ideas to an audience. For some, the pleasure of having a responsive, appreciative audience is the biggest reason for choosing the subject. Others may not wish to appear on stage at all but will enjoy the prospect of designing sets or costumes or rigging lights or sound equipment. Everyone will find something that will interest and challenge them and all will have an important part to play in whatever project you are working on.

Drama is about working with other people

Working as part of a team is something that draws people to the subject. It is also a skill that attracts prospective employers, as the Remember box shows.

Remember

A qualification in Drama demonstrates that you have:

- shown creativity and imagination
- worked with others constructively
- worked to, and met, tight deadlines
- learnt to communicate effectively
- interpreted your own and other people's ideas and realised them.

A *A modern production of a Greek tragedy using masks*

As you work in your group you will learn to share ideas and to offer and take criticism constructively. Unlike many other subjects, in GCSE Drama you are not alone. Sometimes you will have to work under pressure to meet firm deadlines and this can be made less daunting by having the support of others in your group. This is both a comfort and a responsibility. It means that, in return, you will need to give support to others by being reliable, turning up on time for rehearsals and by making sure that lines are learnt or that costumes or sound effects are ready on time. Throughout this book you will see that group working is stressed in every chapter and this is because the success of a drama performance depends entirely on collaboration and teamwork.

■ Drama is about learning new skills

Drama is not just about acting. There are other important areas of skill to be learnt, involving technical and design elements. Though you may start with one area that attracts you, it is possible to branch out and try other skills. In fact, it is an advantage for a lighting technician to know what problems an actor faces on stage, for example, when designing the lighting plot, and all designers need to be aware of the practical limitations of their sets or costumes. You will learn the correct vocabulary and the methods commonly used by professionals, not by memorising lists but by doing. Even the written part of the exam is based on things that you have done or seen while following your course and putting into practice the skills you have acquired.

B *Heptanstall pace-egg play*

Key terms

Mummers' play: a traditional folk play performed usually at Christmas and involving characters such as St George.

Pace-egg play: similar to a mummers' play but performed in the North of England, often on Good Friday.

kerboodle

How GCSE Drama is assessed

Drama is a practical subject that involves teamwork. It covers a wide range of presentation skills.

There are three parts to the assessment:

- Process – your teacher will mark you on your understanding of skills and their development as you work on a project.
- Presentation – you will be marked by your teacher and/or an AQA moderator on your skills' presentation in a final performance of a piece of work. This might be an acting performance, or the presentation of make-up or lighting.
- Written paper – your written examination will test you on what you have done during your course.

Unit 2: Practical work

None of these assessments should cause you any stress or difficulty if you follow the advice in this book. Just complete the practical work and keep notes on what you have done, and why you did it in that particular way, and you will be fine. Your teacher will be keeping notes on your progress so it will be important for you to show that you know and understand what you are doing. Most importantly:

- Show commitment to your group and the project.
- Carry out research for yourself and share it.
- Listen to advice and criticism and act upon it.
- Set targets to ensure the work progresses effectively.

The practical presentation is like any presentation in front of others. It is natural that you might feel nervous. Just think of it as being proof of your excitement and a sign that you want to do well. If you are a performer, take a few deep breaths and go for it – make it your best. If you are a designer or a technician, prepare thoroughly and carefully. When you try your hardest nobody can expect more of you and you will even surprise yourself and gain confidence for next time.

Unit 1: Written paper

The written paper should not offer any surprises and will be based entirely on practical work you have done or seen as part of your course. It will be organised in three sections:

- Section A is a compulsory question based on the practical work you have done during the course.
- Section B is based on the study and performance of a scripted play as part of your course.
- Section C is based on the study of a live theatre performance you have seen.

Objectives

In this section you will learn:

how GCSE Drama is assessed

that the exam is based on what you do and see during your course.

Remember

'You're so lucky to be able to perform like that,' said a fan to a brilliant performer.

'Thank you,' replied the performer, 'and the more I practise the luckier I seem to be.'

Remember

Unit 1, the written paper, is not a separate part of the exam. It is there to test your knowledge and understanding of all the practical work you have done and seen.

You must answer Section A Question 1 and **one** other question, from either Section B or Section C. Here you will have a choice of two questions. Whatever your option choices you will have questions that you can answer.

Plan ahead

It will make sense for you, from the very start of your course, to be thinking about the kinds of question you will answer in Unit 1, the written paper. From your very first lesson you will be learning new vocabulary and approaches to Drama. Keep notes of these after each lesson. At times when you have completed a project, organise your notes in a way that makes sense and will fit in with the kinds of questions you might be asked. You will be given ideas on what you will need to know in each chapter. Whether you organise the points in lists, spider diagrams or even pictures will depend on what works best for you, but do keep up to date. A few notes made often will get you into good habits and it is actually easier than leaving it all to build up. These notes and plans will help you revise just before the written exam and will help you to keep your memories of the practical work fresh in your mind.

> **Study tip**
>
> Remember that Drama is a practical subject and that you should study scripted plays and live theatre performances from a practical point of view. Look at them through the eyes of someone with your practical skills and knowledge.

A *Students at Millthorpe School, York, performing* **Oliver!**

How to get the best out of this book

Whenever you start a new course the amount you have to learn always seems daunting. Do not worry. This book is to give you help and confidence. It will guide you towards other support materials that have been prepared to go with this book.

- First, dip in and look at the chapters that interest you most.
- Notice that the chapters are arranged in sets of pages called 'spreads'.
- Work your way through one spread at a time.
- Follow up the suggestions and apply them to your own work.
- Take note of the various boxes such as the ones on this spread. They are there to help you.

Range of practical options

AQA GCSE Drama offers a wide range of practical options in three areas:

Objectives

In this section you will learn:

how to get the best out of this book

about the range of options available

how the book tackles the different options.

Performance

Design

Technical

Performance	Design	Technical
1 Devised thematic work	6 Set design	12 Lighting
2 Acting performance	7 Costume	13 Sound
3 Improvisation	8 Make-up	14 Stage management
4 Theatre in education	9 Properties	
5 Physical theatre	10 Masks	
	11 Puppets	

Obviously, it would take fourteen separate books to cover everything in detail, so we have based the student book on the five performance skills, which have also been the more popular choices for candidates. The design and technical options are all linked to each of these. This means that if you are, say, a set designer, you can look at the set design sections of all five options and find ideas and advice on how best to develop your skills. Also, you may be in a group of performers without anyone offering design or technical skills to support you. By looking at

Key terms

These boxes give definitions of words that may be new to you. Learn them as you will need to use them in your work. Learn to spell them correctly for the written paper.

A *Calderdale High School students perform their pace-egg play annually on Good Friday*

those sections in your main chapter you should have some ideas on how to prepare costumes or set for your performance. You might even find that you have discovered a new skill that you can develop for assessment.

Everyone has to offer two practical options for the exam. You will need to study at least one scripted play as part of your new course. This can be done through a practical option or as a study of a live production you have visited. This will enable you to answer a second question in Unit 1, the written paper. Ideally, it would be best to try as many options and study as many productions as you can because this will give you a wider experience and understanding of the way in which all the different skills contribute to putting on a drama production.

◯◯ links

www.hebdenbridge.co.uk/features/pace-egg.html

Study tip

These boxes are written by experienced examiners. Each box will give you some helpful advice. The tip from this box is:

Always take notice of the blue boxes, they will point you in the right direction!

Activity

These boxes suggest activities you might do in the classroom or at home. Here is one to get you started.

1 Turn to Chapter 5. Read the first spread. You will discover the basics of TIE. Turn to pages 100–101 on costume design. This will tell you what you have to do if you wish to offer costume design for the examination and how you might apply it to a TIE production.

Remember

Drama is what you make of it. It may seem difficult at times, but if you give it your best effort you will enjoy it and feel the satisfaction of having achieved something important. Good luck with it!

When you choose this option for your Controlled Assessment task, you will prepare and perform a piece of work based on a theme which you and your group have chosen. It will have both scripted and original work in it and will give a very wide scope for your performance and design/technical skills. You will also be able to use the work to answer questions in Section A of Unit 1, the written paper.

If you look at the brochures describing the work coming to your local theatres, you will find many examples of professional companies which devise and perform their own work. Look closely at the page from a brochure from The Point in Eastleigh.

Friday 19th September – 7.30pm

Photograph credit: Kristina Gonzales

The Awake project

A new international production in progress

A multi-talented international cast of actors, musicians, dancers, jugglers and acrobats presents the only UK preview of an exciting new theatre production. Christopher Sivertsen, former long-standing member of Poland's award-winning Song of the Goat theatre, has assembled an impressive ensemble of performers to create, over several months in several countries, a new work exploring questions of life and health using text, movement and live music.

The company has spent five days working in the Point's theatre and now invites you to join them for this very special presentation which will be followed by a discussion.

www.awakeproject.com

Tickets: All seats £5
Duration: approximately 60 minutes
Recommended age: 14+

This is a POINT10 project.

the**point** EASTLEIGH

Photo one: Pelle Holst, Oliviero Papi, Maria Sendow and Satchie Noro
Photo two: Oliviero Papi and Maria Sendow
Photo three: Pelle Holst, Oliviero Papi, Maria Sendow and Satchie Noro

box office **023 8065 2333**

 A page from a brochure for The Point, Eastleigh

Note that the Awake project has:

- an **ensemble** of performers with a variety of talents
- a theme (life and health)
- text
- musical elements
- movement elements.

All these are characteristics of devised work and will result in brand-new and exciting work.

Companies which produce this vibrant and thoughtful work all devise in a different way and use different starting points. They take account of the skills of the company and so will you when you come to devise your own work. They also have a real passion to investigate and develop their **stimulus**. The fact that they chose their starting point or theme means that they feel strongly about it and have a viewpoint which they wish to communicate to an audience. When you choose your theme make sure that you are committed to the points you want to put across to the audience.

Getting started

Volcano Theatre Company from the UK, in preparing their work *i-witness*, were inspired by the writings of WG Sebald and used video, physicality and performance skills to explore 'a world full of the echoes and whisperings of the past'.

New International Encounter (NIE) is an international company which produce work using a variety of languages, musicians on stage and many theatrical styles. Their work *End of Everything Ever* uses true stories and accounts of *Kindertransport* and follows the trials of one child.

Look at their website to investigate their work.

Work based on well-known plays is also devised by theatre companies:

- Frantic Assembly's adaptation of *Othello* mixes movement, design, text and cinematic soundtrack to investigate the themes of prejudice, danger and fear. You can find out about how this company develop their work by looking at their website and their resource packs, especially the one for Stockholm.
- The Nuffield Theatre Company have devised a new piece *The Coast of Mayo*, inspired by their own production of *The Playboy of the Western World*. The actors had the experience of working on both the scripted and the devised piece.

Key terms

Ensemble: a group of people working together; everyone makes an equal contribution and there is no 'starring role'.

Stimulus (plural stimuli): the starting-point for a devised work; the idea, image or object that sparks off your work.

Did you know ??????

In the Second World War, Jewish children were sent abroad from Nazi Germany. That was called *Kindertransport*.

Activity

1. *Kindertransport* was when Jewish children were sent abroad from Nazi Germany during the Second World War. You can research the play called *Kindertransport* by Diane Samuels and a production of this play by Shared Experience. The innovative company bring new and exciting theatre skills in their adaptations of well know texts. See www.sharedexperience.co.uk

kerboodle

There are many themes you could choose to inspire your devised work, so you need to make sure that all your group is interested in the theme you choose, and that you have something to say on the subject. It is important that you put your ideas across to the audience, using both elements of text and original work.

Perhaps you will be inspired by a poem you have enjoyed or by a group of poems on a theme that you are studying. Maybe a novel you are reading suggests a theme that you feel could be developed theatrically, or an issue dealing with environmental matters moves or concerns you. An article in a newspaper or a series of letters on a problem page in a magazine could all be the basis for a unique piece of theatre. In all aspects of your life be aware of ideas which you could investigate.

One way of choosing a theme is to look at a play which you are working on for a different part of this course. In the activities, you will see examples of popular plays and themes.

A *Students from William Parker Sports College performing* **Blue Remembered Hills**

Activities

1. Investigate the theme of childhood and changing relationships of friends and enemies. Try a movement sequence based on playground games to get you started. Look at the poem *Tich Miller*, by Wendy Cope.

2. Investigate the theme of war. Look at *Blue Remembered Hills*, by Dennis Potter. Use sections of this play in a piece on war and its effects on those at home. Improvise some scenes with the parents of the children in the play. Look at *Spies*, by Michael Frayn, for another view of children during the war. This is written as a flashback from the point of view of a character now grown up. You could try to flash forward from the end of *Blue Remembered Hills* to improvise scenes of the children in the future facing up (or not) to what they have done.

Study tip

Keep a research file on everything that could be included in your work but do not be afraid to discard some of it. It's better to have too much material than too little.

Activities

3 Look at *The Caucasian Chalk Circle*, by Bertolt Brecht. Investigate the theme of war from the point of view of the refugee. Grusha has to leave her home because of the war and has to keep a child safe. Look at this situation in the modern world. You could include video material of war situations and audio reports of what people think about refugees. You may find material in newspapers or someone you know may have personal experiences to relate. Compare this to Grusha's situation – begging for milk, escaping from soldiers, being rejected by her family.

4 Work on the play *Hannah and Hanna*, by John Retallack, which deals with refugees today.

5 Another theme you could work on is that of adoption. *The Caucasian Chalk Circle* asks the question 'Who is the real mother?' and looks at the position of an outsider.

6 Look at the poem *So You Think I'm a Mule*, by Jackie Kay, who is a black woman adopted by a white Glaswegian couple. This could lead you on to work on justice, class and prejudice.

B *This scene shows the reaction of Hannah (left) to the refugee Hanna (right)*

In *Sepia and Song*, by David Foxton, there are two plays which use the documentary style to put across fact and opinions. *I was a Good Little Girl* is about the suffragettes struggling for the vote, and *Titanic* investigates the sinking of the ship.

Oh! What a Lovely War (Theatre Workshop) is a wonderful example of **documentary**-style theatre that puts its points across about how the First World War resulted in the deaths of millions. If you are attempting documentary work, or even a documentary section in your devised work, it is a good idea to look at this play to see how the **newspanel** is used together with projections, songs from the period and acting and dancing to make its points.

Key terms

Documentary: putting factual information across to the audience.

Newspanel: written messages flashing across a screen during the play, perhaps giving facts that the audience would find difficult to take in if they couldn't see them.

Resources

As well as all the printed material you have access to, your greatest inspiration will be the live theatre you see. In every production there will be something which works really well, and very often an idea you can use and develop when you get back into your own performance space.

You will be writing notes about the production you've seen and analysing the success of the performances and the design/technical elements, saying what happened on stage and why certain moments were effective. Also keep a file of ideas which inspired you.

When you read a novel it has an effect on your own writing; music you hear and art you see influence your work in these areas; similarly productions you see inspire your own drama, especially in devised work where you can use a variety of styles and ideas.

Small-scale touring productions are designed to fit into a small performance space and pack into a van. Therefore they can be adapted to fit your school studio space. A **composite set** can be used in many ways and lit to suggest different locations.

If you see a **gauze** used effectively, try to set one up. It is not too expensive to buy a gauze or you could borrow one from your local theatre. Change a scene downstage for one upstage of the gauze by cross-fading lights from downstage to upstage. Try projecting onto it. Notice how projections or video or PowerPoint inserts are used in productions.

Experiment with entrances and exits and try out your work in a variety of stage forms (see page 47).

(see page 47)

Study tip

When you get into your performance space, try to reproduce moments from a production that worked well. This will help you to remember what you saw when writing your notes and to realise that you can reproduce ideas you have seen.

Key terms

Composite set: one set used throughout the production, designed to accommodate all locations and needs.

Gauze: also known as scrim, gauze is a coarse-weave fabric which appears transparent when the scene behind it is lit; sharkstooth is the most opaque.

A *Actress on stage with live video of herself*

◾ Skills

Your other main resource is the skills of the people in your group so start off by writing a CAN DO list and add everything you have learnt in all the drama you have done. Don't leave anything out, as it could all be useful in devised work.

Your CAN DO list could contain any of the following:

- Effective tableaux – you could re-create a photograph or comic strip effect
- Physical theatre – could be used in a comedy sequence
- Stepping out from the action – direct address to the audience to make a point or move the action on
- Improvising naturalistic scenes – to show the development of a character
- Performance of text
- Acting and interpreting a character
- Dance or movement sequences – to create a mood or tell a story
- Mime
- Use of masks
- Theatre from other periods – Greek chorus work, Commedia dell' Arte
- Different narrative techniques – narrator, flashbacks, interviews.

You will have many more to add to your own list, but do not forget individual skills that members of your group may have and see if you can use them in your work.

There may be singers and musicians amongst you, or dancers and jugglers. Someone may have photographic skills which could be used to create projections, or someone may be able to make and edit video effectively.

- A solo violin could evoke a poignant moment.
- Tap-dancing a rhythm could suggest gunfire.
- A stand-up comedian would be great at direct address to the audience.
- Martial arts experts could choreograph a movement sequence.

There is no end to the skills you could use in devising your new work – just be sure you do not lose sight of what it's all about.

B *NIE performance*

To give you a feel for devised work, take a basic theme and split up the class to produce a short piece involving everyone and using a variety of skills. The theme is the single word 'despair', which gives plenty of scope.

You will need to divide up into small groups. One group should work on each of the following:

- a set which suggests the theme to the audience
- lighting which will evoke the mood
- a soundtrack which can include live or recorded sound
- images to be projected as a slide show, using equipment such as a **gobo** or **gel**
- a costume which will enhance the theme and which someone in the group will wear
- collecting or making suitable props
- design a make-up or make a mask
- a movement/dance sequence
- some text
- a rehearsed, improvised scene.

You may also add anything else you might like to include. This will depend on the interests of your class but try to cover as many as possible and have at least two people in each group. It might be a good idea to work in a skills area you haven't tried before.

Some points to consider

If you are working on the set you will have to define your performance space and use whatever is available to you. Look especially at fabrics and experiment with creating a variety of levels. Think about colour and texture and make sure there is space for the performers.

The lighting team will need to consult with the set designers. Try to use the minimum number of lanterns, light from unusual angles, try out gobos and different coloured gels.

It might be useful to create your costume on a member of your team and then you will know immediately what it looks like. Make sure it is possible to get on and off and is comfortable to wear. Experiment with a variety of materials, think about spraying and painting and do not forget accessories.

Some examples of text

Chorus speech from *King Oedipus*:

> Sorrows beyond all telling:
> Sickness rife in our ranks, outstripping
> Invention of remedy – blight
> On barren earth,
> And barren agonies of birth –
> Life after life from the wild-fire winging
> Swiftly into the night.
>
> *Sophocles, trans EF Watling*

An extract from *Metamorphosis*

> O God, he thought, what an exhausting job I've picked on! Travelling about day in, day out. It's much more irritating work than doing the actual business in the warehouse, and on top of that there's the trouble of constant travelling, of worrying about train connections, the bed and irregular meals, casual acquaintances that are always new and never become intimate friends. The devil take it all!
>
> *Franz Kafka, trans Martin Secker & Walsburg and Schocken Books Ltd*

Putting your work together

You will need to take time to look at the contributions of all members of the class and then make decisions about how it will be put together. Your teacher will probably be the best person to take a directorial role at this point and shape the work.

The possibilities are endless:

- The movement team could teach their sequence to other people and their work could be an opening or closing sequence.
- You could start in blackout and fade up onto a costumed figure or an empty set.
- Is the soundtrack playing at this point? Is it playing throughout the whole piece or at significant moments?
- Is a dancer wearing a mask or is an actor appearing in appropriate make-up?
- How will the text be delivered – by actors on stage, by a single voice or as a chorus? Will the presentation be static or accompanied by movement?

When your work is structured you will need to rehearse this carefully as it may be quite a technical production. You will need to do a full technical and dress rehearsal before you present your work to an audience.

It is a good idea for everyone to keep a full record of the order of the work and the cues. As you will all be involved in the performance get someone to record it so that you can look at it later.

Study tip

Keep a full record of the process as it will be a help when you create your own group work.

Small group devised thematic work

You will have many ideas of a theme you would like to investigate, which will be challenging to work on and which will give you the chance to develop and improve your skills.

Try the theme of money inspired by the poem *Money (rant)*, by Benjamin Zephaniah. Here is the first verse, which has many ideas, and the whole poem is packed with themes which you could develop.

Money (rant)

Money mek a Rich man feel like a Big man
It mek a Poor man feel like a Hooligan
A One Parent family feels like some ruffians
An dose who hav it don't seem to care a damn,
Money meks yu friend become yu enemy
Yu start see tings very superficially
Yu life is lived very artificially
Unlike dose who live in Poverty.
Money inflates yu ego
But money brings yu down
Money causes problems anywea money is found,
Food is what we need, food is necessary,
Mek me grow my food
An dem can eat dem money.

First stanza from 'Money (rant)', **City Psalms**, *Bloodaxe Books*

A   *The poet Benjamin Zephaniah*

Now that you are working in a smaller group you will need to be able to use a variety of performance skills and work in different areas. If you have a particular skill, try to find an opportunity to use it.

Activities

1
  a   Consider the rhythm of the poem – will you use this piece in your work? You could create a movement or dance piece using the rhythm or a song on the theme.

  b   Look at the line: 'Money meks yu friend become yu enemy.' There is scope here for an interpretation through dance, improvised scenes, monologues showing changes in relationships or poems based on the theme.

  c   The last three lines could lead you into green issues.

2
  a   Look at other related scripts, such as the 12 August scene from *Oh! What a Lovely War*, in which the characters discuss making money from war, or the envy caused by land ownership in *The Crucible*.

  b   Use scenes from *The Good Person of Szechuan* by Brecht. Can you be good if you have money?

  c   You should make a large spider diagram to record all your ideas at this stage.

Study tip

Look at your CAN DO list and experiment practically with your ideas. Choose a suitable performance style for each idea.

Collect any images and material which will help. Everyone should bring at least one stimulus, for example, a photo, magazine/newspaper article, poem or piece of music.

Structuring your work

When you have tried out all your ideas you will have to organise your separate sections into a piece of work which will keep your audience interested. You will also need to make sure that the point you want to put across is clear. What is your work about?

Throughout the preparation period you need to keep careful notes and records of what you have done. You could keep a written notebook or a series of photographs. You may choose to use sticky notes or loose-leaf sheets which you can swap around until you've got the order right. A slide show of scenes may help to sort out the order of the scenes or even pieces of paper pegged onto a washing line.

Aim for variety in presenting your ideas but make sure that the **transitions** between your scenes or sections are smooth and do not hold the action up. You can do this by having a composite set (see page 73), planning where any costume changes will happen and making sure that something else is happening on stage while changes are taking place. Use **cross-fades** for your lighting rather than blackouts. Save blackouts for when you need them for dramatic reasons.

Make sure that your opening really engages the interest of the audience. Shakespeare did: look for example at the fight scene in *Romeo and Juliet*, the witches in *Macbeth* or the ghost scene at the beginning of *Hamlet*. It doesn't have to be a very busy scene: a solo singer, alone on the stage, or a monologue spoken directly to the audience can be just as engaging.

At the conclusion of your work make sure the point you are hoping to make is clear. What are you hoping to say about money and its effects on people?

- Does it make people selfish? Did you know that the poorest members of society give the greatest percentage of their income to charity?
- Does it cause rifts between family and friends?
- Does it make people create inferior work, just for the money?

It's your work and is unique to you and your group.

Study tip

Everyone in the group should take responsibility for keeping a record of the process and have a copy. You may want to use this work to answer Section A on the written paper.

Key terms

Transition: a change between scenes or sections of your work.

Cross-fade: when one lighting state goes out at exactly the same time as another one comes on.

B   *A Pilot Theatre production meeting*

Focusing on your performance skills

When you perform your work you will want to give your best performance. It's a good idea therefore to let someone watch your work throughout the preparation period. The aim is to communicate your ideas to an audience so the comments of your fellow group members or classmates will be very helpful. The direction from your teacher will be invaluable.

You can get tips and help about:

Characterisation:

- Your character should be believable in scripted or improvised scenes.
- Is your characterisation sustained throughout the section?
- Are you showing the age of the character?

Use of voice:

- Are you clear and is your volume appropriate?
- Is the language appropriate to the role?
- Is your accent accurate and fitting the role?

Use of movement:

- Are you showing the mood and status of the character?
- Are you in the best place on stage?
- Are your dance movements accurate?
- Have you thought about rhythm, extensions and positions on stage?

A *The Orange Tree Theatre, Richmond, doing vocal warm-up rehearsals*

You may find that you are needed to play a variety of roles in this work and draw upon dancing, acting and musical skills. You may be working alone delivering a monologue or singing a solo or working with a partner in a dance sequence. You could be acting a scripted extract or performing a choral piece with the whole group.

You will need to concentrate throughout and be completely prepared. You will have to be in character from the moment you enter the scene. Have a clear written outline of the order of scenes during the rehearsals and be in the right place at the right time.

Study tip

When your work is in its final state make sure that you use your rehearsal time effectively.

At the end of each session make notes about what you will rehearse next time. It is very tempting to start at the beginning each time. This will mean that certain scenes will be neglected and maybe that some people in the group will be very bored if you never get round to their scenes.

Make sure that you are fluent in all your lines and movements. If you have solo moments, you need to thoroughly rehearse and ask for help with musical moments if you need pointers. If you are performing a monologue, try recording it onto video and see if you are creating the impression you are aiming for, or ask someone to watch and give you notes on your voice, movement and facial expressions. Record movement, dance or fight sequences so that you can get a sense of your use of space.

If you are involved in improvised work, make sure that you have created a believable character. If you are performing an extract from a scripted piece, read the whole play so that you have a full understanding of the character you are playing.

When you perform, your audience should be entertained and be aware of the point of view you have of your theme.

Give your work a title and create a poster or simulate a brochure page advertising your devised work.

Company Gavin Robertson in association with makin projects present

spittoon

Saturday 27 September 7.30pm
Tickets £11, £10 (concessions),
£9 (supporters)

When Sherriff Jim Daggart springs jailbird Jack Valentine to team up in search of Mexican bandit, Tico, and the lost loot from a bank job in Montery, then it's time for the enigmatic stranger to lend a hand ... enigmatically, of course. Oh ... and Laddie the invisible dog! And his horse, Trigger. Oh ... that's not the dog's horse, that's Jim Daggart's horse.

As hunters and hunted head north towards the Texan border, it's only a matter of time before the two teams cross paths – and double cross each other! Twice!

B   **Spittoon** *is a parody and a homage to the Western in all its forms*

2.6 Option 6: Set design

As the work develops

From the moment the theme is chosen you need to begin collecting a folder of images and ideas. These will be very important to the rest of the group and could work as a stimulus for performance work. See how the mood is developing and think about colours and materials which you would like to use. The basic components of set design are **flats** and **rostra** and you need to experiment with ideas to see what effects you can create.

Activity

1. a Find a cardboard box and paint it black inside (or cover the inside of it with black paper).
   b Cut out a series of rectangles and paint them white. Add a tab at the back so that they are free-standing.
   c Collect or make a series of small boxes and paint them white.
   d Now arrange them in the box. You will have a huge number of possibilities.
   e Put in a cut-out figure to get some sense of scale.
   f Try lighting your arrangements either with lanterns or with torches.
   g Try different combinations of coloured gels and light from different directions.
   h Take photographs of the different combinations to discuss with your group.

This will give you some sense of the moods you can create and, if you find an arrangement that seems to be both suggestive of the mood or theme and practical for actors and audience, it could be the basis of your design.

Objectives

In this section you will learn to:

- be part of a creative team
- use your performance space to the benefit of both actors and audience
- create a mood and atmosphere suitable to the chosen theme
- work closely with any other design/technical people in your group
- make a scale model of your set
- create the set as near as possible to your design
- keep and present details of the progress of your ideas.

Key terms

Flat: a light wooden frame covered in scenic canvas, plywood or hardboard which can be painted to suit your work.

Rostrum (plural rostra): a portable platform which you can use to create interesting levels.

Sight line: what your audience can see on the stage; sit at the extreme ends of the front row to work it out.

A Set design incorporating graffiti on a red brick wall

B   *In* **End of Everything Ever**, *by NIE Theatre, the whole design was based on a wooden wardrobe*

In *End of Everything Ever*, NIE Theatre used a wardrobe for entrances into interiors and, as can be seen in this image, as a train window as the child begins her journey away from her family.

During rehearsals

By now you will have finalised your basic design and begun to make your scale model.

Use the scale 1:25. Make your ground plan, taking into account the form of stage you are using (see page 47) and pay attention to **sight lines**. The simplest way of doing this is to mock up your set and audience seating, get people to walk the set and others to sit at the extreme points of the seating. When you are satisfied that the set works put your sight lines onto your ground plan. Then make sure that the actors are aware of this. When you tape the set out on the floor of your space, tape in the sight lines too.

You will need to be flexible because the nature of devised work means that new ideas will be buzzing around throughout the preparation period, but try to keep the basic design intact otherwise you will be making your scale model at a very late stage for your assessment.

Be aware, for example, that there might be a need for projections at some point so experiment with different types of screen and different directions of projecting. You will be able to advise the group of the best way of getting the points across and be able to use the screen as part of your design. If you are working with a lighting designer you must consult with him or her.

By the dress rehearsal you may be able to just watch and enjoy. Take photos of your work under the lighting.

> **Remember**
>
> Take into account live productions you have seen in the theatre and be aware of any ideas that you could use and adapt.

> **Study tip**
>
> At the technical rehearsal, make careful notes and include these in your records. This will show how you are able to come up with practical solutions to solve any problems that may crop up.

2.7 Option 7: Costume design

▇ As the work develops

You will be involved in the choice of the theme your group will work on so make sure that you keep a file of images that suggest the theme. You may need to research period or style and your ideas may form the stimulus for performance work.

You will have some idea of what you want your design to say but remember also that it will need to be practical. It will have to fit the performer and be comfortable. Make sure also that it meets the needs of what the performer will have to do on stage and that it is durable enough to last the run.

Objectives

In this section you will learn to:

be part of a creative team

use your designing skills to show the mood and atmosphere of the work

respond suitably to the needs of the piece

experiment with fabrics, colours and textures

make one costume and design the others

keep and present details of the progress of your work.

Activity

1. a Look at your notes from productions you have seen and note any ideas you would like to use.

   b Come up with abstract ideas which suggest the theme.

   c If you are working on the Money project, design outrageous costumes showing excess.

   d Cinderella's ugly sisters could be an inspiration for catwalk designs.

   e Collect a variety of fabrics but do not limit yourself.

   f Make designs using string, plastic, painted canvas, egg boxes.

   g Get hold of some old hats and remodel them suggesting the theme.

   h Make sure you have the measurements of the people in your group.

   i Find out what your budget is and research markets and fabric shops.

A From Oh! What a Lovely War *theatre workshop*

During rehearsals

In devised work the performers will often have to play more than one role or show more than one skill. As a costume designer you will be able to help the performance considerably by creating or designing costumes which will allow for quick changes and will capture the character perfectly to make the role seem more convincing.

You may decide to design a basic costume which will be worn by all performers. Then you will be able to design additions for each actor to use to show their different roles.

In *Oh! What a Lovely War* (Theatre Workshop), the horrific story of the First World War is told through an end of the pier show of that period and uses songs of the time.

Look at the photographs from a production of *Oh! What a Lovely War*. The characters are all wearing pierrot costumes in black and white with ruffles and pom-poms. The costumes suggest a uniform and are worn throughout the play. The different items, such as hats and other pieces of uniform, are added during the play to set the scene and differentiate the characters as the actors play a variety of parts.

At the technical rehearsal make sure that your performers know exactly where their costumes will be for any changes and that they have rehearsed their changes. Be there to help if they need it.

At the dress rehearsal take photos of your work in action.

> **Study tip**
>
> Make notes of any alterations you need to make.

B *The pierrot costumes with their prominent pom-poms*

2.8 Option 8: Make-up

As the work develops

You will be able to design two contrasting make-ups so you will need to discuss with the rest of the group (especially other design/technical people) and the director, when the make-up will be most relevant to the theme.

Objectives

In this section you will learn to:

be part of a creative team

be aware of the theme and how your skills can enhance and illustrate it

apply make-up effectively

be aware of how it will look on stage.

Activity

1 a Experiment with different types of make-up.

   b Research different products.

   c Research a production of the musical *Cats* for inspiration.

   d Try out ideas either on yourself or someone else.

   e Work with the costume designer on choice of colours.

   f Look at the effects you are creating under stage lighting, so that you are not suddenly disappointed by the results.

∞ links

www.stagemakeuponline/bennye

During rehearsals

You will need to be flexible, as the structuring of the work may mean that you will have to create a make-up change during the performance. Make sure that your kit is in good order and make sure that you have a backstage area to do changes.

You will also need to be responsible for any body make-up. You will be able to enhance your designs with the use of wigs and/or hairstyles so make sure that you discuss your ideas throughout the rehearsal period with the performers and other designers.

At the technical rehearsal make sure you can rehearse any make-up changes. Don't forget to clean the make-up off properly and allow time for this.

At the dress rehearsal run everything as though it is an actual performance.

Study tip

Always try to have rehearsal time to try out your ideas. You can do lots of sketches and diagrams, which will help you explain your ideas and will provide evidence of how your ideas developed.

A *Make-up can add a striking effect to your production*

2.9   Option 9: Properties

As the work develops

You will need to keep track of the work so that you can suggest ideas for props you would like to make in order to show your skills. You will be able to design and make two props for the production and will also need a full props list.

- Collect your materials together.
- Keep a props list of what you may need to borrow or hire.
- Make detailed sketches of the two props you will make.
- Discuss the needs of the props with the performers who are going to use them.
- Be alert to opportunities to show your skills.

Activity

1 Look at the photographs from *Oh! What a Lovely War* on the Costume page.

a Write a props list for this scene. There are many different items. You would have to research this and find out how to get hold of all items or hire them.

b What props could you make for this scene? The gun would be a good choice, as research would be necessary.

c If you were in charge of props you would need to organise hats and pieces of uniform. You may decide to make the sergeant's webbing or the flags in the women's scene. There are canes and boaters to be made or sourced and a swagger stick for the sergeant. There are many challenges in other scenes, such as guns and a lavish picnic in the scene where making money from war is discussed.

During rehearsals

Sketch your ideas and discuss them with the rest of the group. Make a detailed props list and check off items when you get hold of them. Find items to stand in as rehearsal props so that the actors get used to using them and you get used to planning where they will be off stage. You will also know how they are **set** and who **strikes** them. If you are hiring or borrowing, keep details so that you can return them efficiently.

Start to make your chosen props as soon as possible as you do not want to be working on them at the last minute and the actors will need to rehearse with them.

At the technical rehearsal, take careful notes of any problems. At the dress rehearsal, take photos of your props in use.

Objectives

In this section you will learn to:

be part of a creative team

be aware of the theme

be aware of the style of the piece and do your research

keep details of everything you will need

work out where you will store your materials and completed props.

A *The Orange Tree Theatre Company familiarise themselves with their props*

Key terms

Setting: putting props on to a set ready for a performance and taking them off again.

Striking: taking props off the set. The whole set is struck at the end of the performance run.

Study tip

Store your work carefully as lost props waste time.

2.10 Option 10: Masks

As the work develops

There is considerable scope for mask-making in devised work. You can interpret the theme and create fantasy and gross characters. You can change the role of the actors and disguise them. If you are working on the Money theme you can show greed and over-indulgence, envy or any character trait through your mask.

Activity

1.
   a Collect images of masks in performance. *The Lion King* will be a good start.
   b Research the early work of Trestle Theatre Company.
   c Collect materials you could use — be very creative here.
   d Practise making simple face masks to fit the performers.
   e Practise making masks that fit on the performers' heads – collect some old hats as a basis for experiment.
   f Try out different textures and colours and look at them under stage lighting.
   g Work with your costume designer in terms of style/materials and colour.

During rehearsals

Try out your ideas and work on your sketches and basic models so that you can discuss your ideas and keep a record of how your ideas are progressing. Collect your materials together and experiment with different ways of using them and how they can be fixed together. Keep records of your methods. Make sure that masks are comfortable and secure in performance. Be aware of what the performers are doing and work with them. The style of mask you design will depend on whether the actor needs to speak in it or not. Your masks need to enhance the performance, not inhibit it by being difficult to wear.

At the technical rehearsal, check where your masks will be off-stage and how they will be stored. At the dress rehearsal, make sure that you take photographs of your work in performance.

Objectives

In this section you will learn to:

be part of a creative team

research the theme to come up with as many ways of interpreting it as possible

design two contrasting masks

consider the comfort of the actors

construct durable masks.

∞links

www.trestle.org.uk

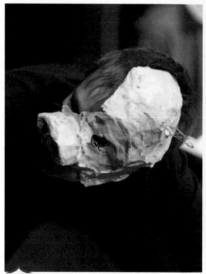

A *An actor wearing a pig mask in an* **Animal Farm** *production*

Study tip

Make sure the actors know how to wear the mask in order to do your work justice and store your masks carefully.

2.11 Option 11: Puppets

As the work develops

If you have seen puppets in any productions, keep careful notes of their construction, type and effect and of how the puppeteer manipulated them. *War Horse* (from the novel by Michael Morpurgo) at the National Theatre used full-sized puppets of horses with three puppeteers to manipulate each one.

Puppets were also used at the National Theatre in the adaptation of Philip Pullman's *His Dark Materials*. They represented the daemons (spirits) of the characters and the puppeteers' skills were part of the performance – although the audience's attention is, of course, focused on the puppets. Look up this production on www.nationaltheatre.org.uk. Try the backstage pages and department profiles.

Activity

1.
  a. Research different types of puppet and keep photographs and sketches.
  b. Decide what type of puppet you will make and how it will be used in the piece.
  c. Collect materials you might use – you can be as adventurous as you like.
  d. It may be that you choose to represent an idea or a gross and exaggerated character in the Money project.
  e. Often a puppet can do what an actor can't on stage.

During rehearsals

Start constructing your puppet as soon as possible so that you can experiment and perfect the manipulation of it. Rehearse in the scenes in which it will appear, even if it isn't ready, so that the other performers will be aware of how it is going to appear. They may have suggestions for further uses for it, so be flexible and adaptable.

At the technical rehearsal, get someone else to make notes if you are performing. At the dress rehearsal, get someone to take photos as a record of your work.

Objectives

In this section you will learn to:

be part of a creative team

design a puppet which enhances the theme of the work

show why you have chosen to design the type of puppet you have

discuss with the others in the group how the puppet will work in the piece

be prepared to operate the puppet yourself as part of the work.

Study tip

If your puppet needs props, make them too, and consult with others if you need music or sound effects. If you are making shadow puppets you also need to construct the screen and organise the lighting.

∞ links

www.nationaltheatre.org.uk

A *Puppets can be integral to the value of a production*

2.12 Option 12: Lighting

As the work develops

As a lighting designer in devised work you will have the opportunity to develop a very creative approach. You may be able to light in a variety of styles such as naturalistic, strong side or overhead lighting for dance or abstract moments and with projections. You will be able to interpret the theme through your lighting. You can change the mood of the piece and keep up the pace of the work by operating efficiently.

Activity

1. a. If you are working with a set designer work with him or her on the exercise on Set design on page 24. If not, do the exercise yourself.

   b. Cut holes in the top and sides of the box to light through and try different gels.

   c. Keep notes of all your ideas and make sketches.

   d. Check that all equipment available to you is in good working order.

   e. Research companies which will sell and hire equipment and effects. What is available?

During rehearsals

You will need to be flexible throughout and look out for opportunities to use your skills. You should be aware of the colour and texture of the set, the colours and fabrics of the costumes and the different styles. You may have to use projections, so work out where the projector will be placed and how you will need to modify your lighting.

At the technical rehearsal, work out how you will be cued, finalise your cue sheet and keep notes of any changes. At the dress rehearsal work as though it is a performance.

Objectives

In this section you will learn to:

be part of a creative team

use a variety of lanterns and effects to show your understanding and versatility

experiment with colour in relation to costume and set

write a detailed plot of your lighting

write a detailed cue sheet.

A *If there are any projections being used you will need to check your lighting works with them*

Controlled Assessment

2.13 Option 13: Sound

As the work develops

Activity

1. a Collect and record songs appropriate to the theme.
   b Collect and record music appropriate to the theme.
   c Note any moments in productions you have seen which you would like to try out.
   d Be aware of the needs of the performance – any dance numbers or fight sequences.
   e Try composing and recording with others in your group.
   f Experiment with putting a sound track together.
   g Experiment with recording individual voices and choral work. Add a backing track.
   h Research sound effect CDs and try recording your own effects.

Objectives

In this section you will learn to:

be part of the creative team

research the theme and pre-recorded music available

collect together equipment that is available to you

respond to the production and be prepared to develop a variety of styles

record, set up and operate music and effects.

During rehearsals

You will have the chance to make all sorts of ideas work. You may be able to use personal microphones or microphones on stands. You will be able to decide where your speakers should be placed for maximum effect. Some sounds may be effective coming from behind the audience. Keep the cue sheet up to date and keep copies of everything you record. If you are recording performers in your group make sure you set aside time to do this early on in the rehearsal period so that you will have time to edit and refine it. Keep a clear plan of where everything will be and take note of health and safety issues. Where will your equipment be and where will you operate it from? Work with the lighting designer or operator so that you can time cues together. Work together on the opening sequence to establish the mood from the very beginning.

At the technical rehearsal, finalise your cue sheet and make sure you have details of volume, length of the cue and which speakers you will use.

At the dress rehearsal, everything should run as though it is a performance.

Skills study

Research the work of Filter Theatre Company, which is well known for a creative use of sound.

⚭ links

www.filtertheatre.com

A **Water** *by Filter Theatre Company. The sound equipment does not have to be hidden from the audience*

2.14 Option 14: Stage management

As the work develops

You will need to be in control of the whole performance so make sure that you are engaged with the theme and that you are aware of the contributions that everyone else in the group will make. If you are working with technical or design people then you must make sure that they are aware of all changes in the structuring of the work. You also need to be sure that they have time in the rehearsal period to try out their ideas. If there are no other design or technical candidates in your group, then you and the performers will need to make decisions about all these elements.

Activity

1.
  a Keep notes, diagrams and images from the very start. Include the original spider diagram.

  b Organise your notes so that you can remind the group of any areas they are neglecting.

  c Begin to make your prompt copy as soon as possible (see page 83).

  d Make sure that you have accurate copies of the script or text that is being used.

  e Consult with others so that you can tape out the set as soon as possible.

  f Make sure that there is sufficient space backstage for props tables and/or costume changes.

  g Research sources for hiring costumes or lighting effects.

  h Keep an up-to-date cast list (the performers may be playing more than one role).

  i Find out if you have a budget to work with and keep all receipts.

Objectives

In this section you will learn to:

be part of the creative team

list all the equipment you have at your disposal

find out how you will borrow or hire any other equipment

keep constant communication with everyone in the group – write everything down and make copies

take responsibility for rehearsal schedules

check all health and safety issues.

During rehearsals

As soon as you can, organise a **scenario** and make sure that everyone has a copy. However, you will need to be flexible as there may be changes. Provide rehearsal props and furniture for the sake of the actors. This will also help you, as you will be aware of what is on stage at any one time and will not forget to arrange how to strike it. If there are going to be costumes that may be difficult to wear, or complicated changes, suggest using practice clothes. At the end of each rehearsal, plan what you will do next time and, if you are working outside teaching time, draw up a rehearsal schedule. Give everyone a copy.

Key terms

Scenario: the summary or outline of the plot of the play.

Cue to cue: go through the play to all moments when there is any technical change (to lighting, sound or set) and rehearse them.

The technical rehearsal

- Try to have this rehearsal a couple of days before the dress rehearsal, as this will give you some time to sort out any problems.

- Keep a list of contact numbers for your group in case anyone needs to get in touch with you.

- By now your prompt copy should be complete and you need to have recorded all entrances and exits and where performers are on the stage throughout.

- You will also have pencilled in all lighting (LX) cues and sound (FX) cues. You also need music and projection cues and anything else which is relevant.

- Decide where you will be during the performance so that you can cue technical operators and work out your cuing system.

- Go through the play from **cue to cue** and, when you are all satisfied with each one, note the details in your prompt copy in as much detail as possible.

- You may need to rehearse costume changes, complicated entrances and exits and any changes to the set.

> **Did you know** ??????
>
> LX is short for electrics (that is, lighting) and FX for effects (that is, sound).

The dress rehearsal

- Run this rehearsal exactly as a performance.

- If anything goes wrong keep going and sort out the problems later. After all, if something goes wrong in the performance you can't stop and start again.

- Make sure that the opening sequence is worked out so that lighting and sound work together.

- Check that every prop and costume is in place before you start.

- Check that all equipment is in working order.

- Make sure that the backstage area is tidy and safe and make sure that you strike efficiently at the end.

- You will probably be sharing your performance space with other groups, so organise where you are going to keep all your props etc., so that they do not get in anyone else's way.

- You should leave your prompt copy in your performance space, and it should be so clear that anyone should be able to run the show from it.

If all goes according to plan, your performance(s) should be a dream.

> **Remember**
>
> Warn everyone that this will be a long rehearsal and ask the performers especially to be patient.

A *Stage manager at work*

2

The work you do on this Controlled Assessment task will be useful in all elements of this course. Your practical skills will be relevant to all other practical tasks, and you will be able to analyse them and write about them on the written paper.

■ Unit 1: The written paper

The Controlled Assessment Task devised thematic work will be ideal for answering Section A questions. You may be able to give details of your stimulus or starting point and why this theme was chosen. You may also be able to explain how you developed the ideas into a piece of drama.

As you rehearsed your work you will have made improvements and changes and you may be asked to say how these were done and why – and whether they made the work more successful.

There may be the opportunity to analyse the strengths and weaknesses of the whole piece or of your own personal skills.

You will be able to show your understanding of different performance styles and why you chose different styles in your work. You will be able to explain your own contribution to the work.

You can see that it is therefore very important to keep a record of the work you have done. You may do this as a diary, as a series of recordings or as photographs. You could make videos of rehearsals, which will also help you to refine your work. Make sure that you have a recording of your final performance, as this will be great when you come to revise for the written paper.

Design and technical students will have a detailed record of their progress as part of their practical assessment, and this will be an excellent revision tool too.

If you answer this question there will be 40 marks available, and that is half of the marks for the whole paper, so you will have to make sure that you revise the work thoroughly so that you can give plenty of detail.

You will be able to use clearly labelled sketches and diagrams in your answer, so practise these in your revision period.

You will have 45 minutes to write your answer.

■ Unit 2: The Controlled Assessment task

When you have finished this work you will perform it in front of an audience. This could be the rest of your group, friends and relatives, a school assembly or the public. A moderator may be present, and their job is to moderate the marking of your teacher.

All the way through your rehearsal period you should ask for feedback. Someone in your group not involved in a particular scene or section can watch and comment on your work and suggest improvements as could someone from another group. You can also make videos of your work in progress.

> **Study tip**
>
> You may have used a live performance you have seen to inspire this work, so do not forget to revise this if you want to answer a Section C question.

Your teacher will be awarding you a mark for your preparation, so his or her feedback will be very important. You should show an awareness of how you can develop your work, and you should be able to work co-operatively and creatively in the group.

In your final performance you will be assessed on how you use your practical skills to put your ideas across to the audience. In devised work, you will be able to show a variety of skills. Make sure that you choose skills which will help to show your ability. If, for example, you enjoy working with a script then be sure to be involved in those scenes or sections. If you are a talented dancer take responsibility for this aspect of the work.

Your teacher will be crediting:

- your creative approach
- originality
- how you relate text and different styles
- how you sustain the quality of your performance
- your use of voice, movement, gesture, facial expression and how you relate to others on stage.

If you are fully prepared you will really enjoy your performance, and so will your audience.

A *Still from* **Some Trace of Her**, *director Katie Mitchell, National Theatre*

Professional actors spend their lives becoming characters, or people who someone else has created. When you begin to work on a scripted play you will be given many clues as to how to create and portray your role. Some of the characters you perform will have their roots in history. In this chapter we will be looking at how to create a character in a scripted play and the skills and techniques you can apply in order to create that role.

For the acting Controlled Assessment option, you will use a play written by a playwright, learn the lines, and take the words and directions from the page through the rehearsal process to the stage and perform it to an audience.

What professional actors do in rehearsals is attempt to create the roles written by the playwright and the way they do this depends very much on the **period**, **society**, **culture** and **genre** of the play.

Period is the time when the play is set. This is in itself very important to consider because the historical context of the play will have a direct influence on the way in which the characters act.

Society deals with who the people portrayed in the play were and how they lived in this community at this time. The type of characters and their relationships with each other also directly influence the way your character will behave on stage.

Culture deals with the rites and rituals of the particular society represented in the play.

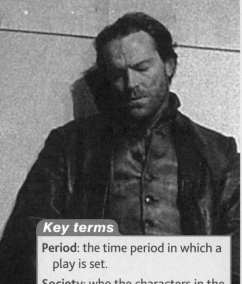

Key terms

Period: the time period in which a play is set.

Society: who the characters in the play are.

Culture: how the characters in the play live their lives.

Genre: the type of production, for example comedy, tragedy, thriller or documentary.

A *Actors from a Royal Shakespeare Company production of* **The Crucible**

Your group will decide the way in which your play is acted. Genre is a category that your play fits into. It could be a comedy, tragedy, thriller, documentary, melodrama or even sometimes a mixture of genres. This is influenced by the nature of the play being studied and prepared for performance and will be linked to the historical period in which the play is set.

Getting started

When people talk about 'drama' they first think of acting plays, and to most people plays mean 'scripts'. When we go to see plays at the theatre, those plays usually begin life as a script. We, as an audience, experience the words and thoughts of the playwright as they breathe life into the characters they shape and create on stage before us.

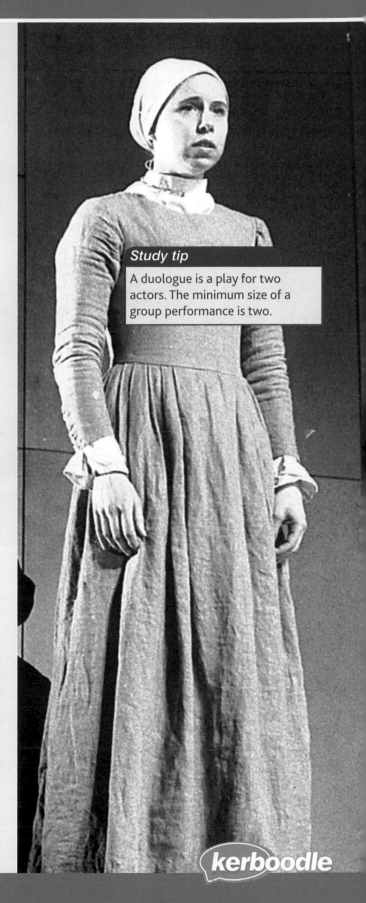

Study tip

A duologue is a play for two actors. The minimum size of a group performance is two.

B *Salem, Massachusetts*

kerboodle

3.1 Looking at the play

How do we begin to act out a scripted play? The first thing to do is to get some idea of the plot of the play and look at some of the characters the playwright has created for us.

The cast list is at the beginning of the play, and this usually includes a cast list of the first night of the performance, when it was performed, and where.

A *Actors in rehearsal for a production of* **Animal Farm**

Once a play is cast the process of rehearsals can begin. Rehearsals can take place over a period of time, but for the purposes of this Controlled Assessment option, the rehearsal period will be approximately 10–12 weeks. Of course, you are not rehearsing as a professional actor does – you have other school commitments – but the process of putting on a play is the same. A great deal of time and hard work and a commitment to the other members of your group is essential.

Your rehearsal process will soon fall into a pattern which will probably include lunchtime and after-school rehearsals, but it will be a pattern that will suit your needs. You may not be required to rehearse at every meeting of the cast, particularly once the play has been **blocked**. You, as a performer, must learn your lines and take direction from the person directing the play. In most cases, this will be your teacher.

Now, you are a member of the cast of the play and once you have been given the name of the character you are to portray, the fun can begin!

Activities

1 Read through the cast list at the beginning of the play. Imagine what the characters are like and see if you can get any clues from the playwright about the characters. What are their ages and what description has the playwright included?

2 Look at the cast list of the first performance of *The Crucible*. Where was it performed, and when?

Study tip

You will receive marks for this aspect of the process, for the Part 1 assessment in your Controlled Assessment option.

Key terms

Blocking: being told by the director where to stand, move or sit as you move through the first reading of the play; you can make notes of these moves in your script to help you to remember them in the next rehearsal.

B   *Director John Malkovich talking through his ideas during rehearsal*

The **director** has the responsibility of pulling all the ideas of all the members of the cast together to create the play. The Duke of Meiningen (1826–1914) was thought to be the first theatre director in the modern sense. Stanislavski founded the Moscow Arts Theatre and Artaud founded The Theatre Live in Paris, and they were both influenced by the style of the Duke in the 1890s.

Modern theatre directors also have to cope with the advances in modern technology and special effects and these, even in the school sense, can be quite sophisticated and enhance the theatrical experience for the audience. Remember, though, it is your individual acting skill that is being assessed, not the production as a whole.

Key terms

Director: the person who tells an actor how and when to do something on stage.

Activities

3   Explore and research your character. Find out if they were someone who actually lived. For the purposes of this project, they probably would have lived and you can find out a great deal about them to help you in portraying your role. Present your findings to the rest of the group.

4   Research Stanislavski and Artaud.

Creating a character

As an example, this chapter focuses on a play called *The Crucible*. However, the skills you will learn and produce here are easily transferable to **any** scripted play. It is the processes that you will try that are important. *The Crucible* was written by Arthur Miller in 1953 and first published in the USA. It is set, however, at a much earlier time, in 1692, in a small community in Salem, Massachusetts. Their ancestors arrived in the New World on the *Mayflower*, but this community developed their own laws and rules for their society and their community to be established. They were 'Puritans' and had a strict code of conduct to live by which was influenced by the Bible.

Did you know ? ? ? ? ?

A crucible is a small melting pot.

Activity

1 Research Salem and the Salem witch trials of 1692.

A **Mayflower II**, *a replica of the ship that took the pilgrims to the New World*

When you begin to create your character you must consider who you are in the play and what is your relationship with the other characters. *The Crucible* has a number of main characters. They include:

- Reverend Parris: Mid-40s, the reverend of the town, not well liked and ambitious
- Abigail Williams: 17, strikingly beautiful, his niece
- Mary Warren: Her friend, subservient, naïve and lonely
- John Proctor: Mid-30s, attractive, strong, a pillar of the community
- Elizabeth Proctor: His wife, a 'covenanted' Christian woman, who has never lied
- Reverend Hale of Beverley: Well-meaning but influenced by his beliefs – blinded by them
- Tituba: Negro slave, scapegoat, dabbles in witchcraft and spells.

Now we go about creating a character. For the purpose of this chapter, we will look at two characters: John Proctor and Abigail Williams.

Study tip

The process of creating the character is focusing here on two main characters but the processes involved are the same for whichever role you are portraying.

Key terms

Hot-seating: the technique of an actor staying in role while answering questions from the audience about the character's thoughts and feelings; the actor can involve the audience by asking the audience for advice.

■ Creating the role of John Proctor

You will have researched the background detail to the play now and explored many aspects of the character as you have 'blocked' the play. John Proctor's first entrance is in Act One. The doomed affair between Abigail and John is clearly established and the subject of much gossip within the community. His desire for contact with Abigail still persists but is against their 'law' and he has committed the sin of adultery. He is a lecher and is accused of this in open court later in the play.

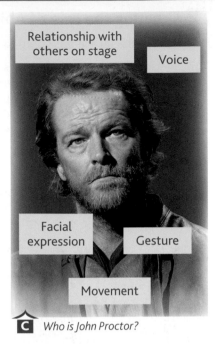

C   *Who is John Proctor?*

Relationship with others on stage

Voice

Facial expression

Gesture

Movement

B   *John Proctor and Abigail Williams in* **The Crucible**

> **Did you know** ??????
>
> A lecher is a man given to lewdness: lustful indecent behaviour. Adultery is sexual unfaithfulness within marriage.

Now we consider John Proctor's first entrance in the play. We have been given clues about him earlier in the scene when the girls were discussing the events in the forest and how Tituba was creating a love potion for Abigail concerning John. Consider the language of the scene and the way the girls react to his entrance. They are afraid of him but also aroused by him, particularly Abigail, who fully believes he has come to Salem to see her.

Next, follow the plan (see Diagram **D**) to help you to build up his character by exploring and creating a character profile.

In exploring his character in this way and analysing what attributes make up his characteristics, you are ready to begin the rehearsal process of developing the character through your research of John Proctor, the man. Now look at the characteristics in Diagram **C** to build up your character profile.

As you begin to create his character, you will ask yourself the following questions:

- ■ What does he do?
- ■ How does he do this?
- ■ Why does he do it in this way?

Now try a **hot-seating** exercise with John Proctor in the chair. Class members can ask the questions as themselves or also be in role.

John Proctor

1. Who is he?

2. What do we know about him?

3. Who are his friends? Why?

4. Who are his enemies? Why?

5. What is his relationship with others in the play?

6. What are his physical characteristics?

7. What are his 'key moments'?

8. What happens to him at the end of the play?

D   *What must we consider?*

Creating the role of Abigail Williams

The next character we are going to consider is Abigail Williams.

Consider the language Abigail uses at the opening of the play. We see here a contrast between her conversation with Reverend Parris and the conversation she has with her friends once he has left the room and gone to speak with the congregation below. She speaks with authority and manipulates the other girls with threats and ultimatums. The other girls are in awe of her. How would you show this when you are creating the role?

E   *Abigail Williams is a strong prescence in* **The Crucible**

Look at Diagram **F** to see how to create her character profile.

Abigail Williams

1. Who is she?

2. What do we know about her?

3. Who are her friends? Why?

4. Who are her enemies? Why?

5. What is her relationship with others in the play?

6. What are her physical characteristics?

7. What are her 'key moments'?

8. What happens to her at the end of the play?

   Who is Abigail Williams?

In exploring Abigail's character in this way and analysing what makes her behave the way she does, you are now ready to begin the rehearsal process. Your detailed research will help you to create the role of Abigail Williams and you will know her before you begin.

In scripted drama there are no insignificant roles. The playwright has constructed the drama to accommodate a number of actors, and they all must play their part for the drama to unfold and the story to be understood by the audience.

All the other characters in *The Crucible* are important. They are responsible for supporting the story and for the development of the underlying themes of greed and revenge which help to shape the drama as it unfolds on stage.

It is not necessary to have as many actors as there are roles. It is common for one actor to play more than one role. You will have to watch out for characters that interact with each other – but it can provide an opportunity for you to use masks or other devices to make the distinction between the two roles.

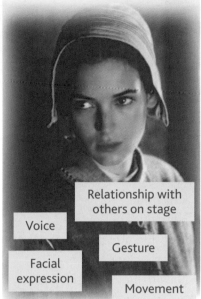

Relationship with others on stage

Voice

Facial expression

Gesture

Movement

G *What must we consider?*

Study tip

Choose a scene or section from the play. Explore what your character is doing, how they are doing it and why they are doing it in that way. This is what you must do for the Section B question on the written examination paper.

H *The characters John Proctor and Abigail Williams in* **The Crucible**

kerboodle

3.3 Option 6: Set design

The place you perform *The Crucible* will influence a great number of things. The performance space must be suitable for the play to be performed, the actors to act and the audience to see, hear and appreciate the play.

For this Controlled Assessment option you are required to create a scale model of the set.

Your work in progress must include:

- diagrams
- drawings of the set
- considerations of methods of building
- set changing
- health and safety factors.

Choose a scene or section from the play that will enable you to meet this challenge. In your planning and research, you will consider a number of performance spaces and the requirements specified by the playwright for the production of *The Crucible*. Some playwrights go into great detail describing what the stage should look like. You will be wise to study these.

Although this work must contribute to a group performance of a scene or section of the play, the work you produce must be your own individual work.

It is not a requirement to realise the set in production but your scale model must be detailed to achieve good results.

A The Crucible, *RSC production, Stratford*

There are a number of different types of performance spaces for you to explore and consider in your design.

An end-on stage (Diagram **B**) is rectangular with the audience on one side. An example of this type of stage is the Lowry Theatre in Salford.

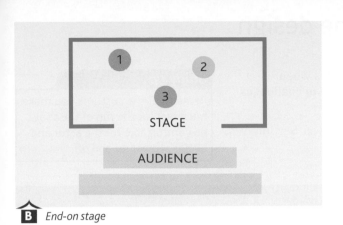

B *End-on stage*

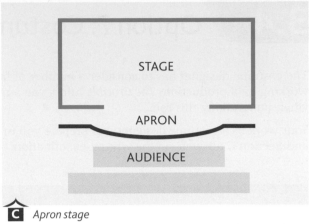

C *Apron stage*

An apron stage (Diagram **C**) is rectangular but the performance space extends beyond the proscenium arch. An example of this type of stage is the Birmingham Rep Theatre.

A thrust stage (Diagram **D**) is one that extends into the audience on three sides and is connected to the backstage area by its up stage ends. An example of a thrust stage can be found at the Swan Theatre in Stratford.

In theatre in the round (Diagram **E**), the audience sits all around the stage. An example of this type of stage is the Royal Exchange, Manchester.

Once you have decided on the type of stage you are going to construct you must decide on your scene.

For example, the opening of Act Two is set in the common room of John Proctor's house (the room in which John Proctor and his family would live). When drawing your ground plans and sketches, pay particular attention to the detail that Arthur Miller gives you. Entrances and exits must be carefully considered. Where will your actors stand whilst they are waiting to come on stage? What sort of view will your audience have of the actors as they perform? What materials will you use to construct your set design and how will your design be realised in performance terms?

You will also need to consider costing, textures, colours, and fabrics in your design and how your design will look when other design elements are considered. Your actors will also need space to move. Don't forget this!

Summary

You will now have:

- knowledge and understanding of the use of space in relation to the actors and the audience

- an awareness of period, creation of mood and atmosphere to different forms of presentation of the scene or section you design.

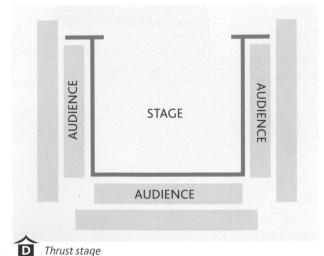

D *Thrust stage*

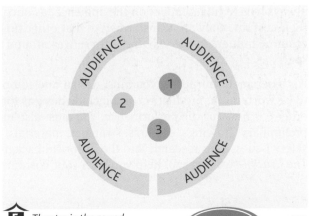

E *Theatre in the round*

3.4   Option 7: Costume design

The costume designer has to consider a number of factors when working on a production. *The Crucible* offers you a range of challenges when undertaking this role.

Your work as a costume designer will prepare you to answer Section A and Section C answers on the written examination.

> **Study tip**
>
> Remember the costume you make must last for the run of the show, be comfortable for the actor and be easy to get on and off.

A   *The court scene in* **The Crucible** *– note Mary Warren's costume*

Costume is the style of dress of a particular place or time and for a particular activity. It can also include accessories. Costume will always have a huge impact on the audience, as once an actor wears their costume they are transformed to that other time and place. The costume influences the way the actor moves around the performance space.

> **Study tip**
>
> Attention to detail helps gain marks in assessment terms so do your research well!

For assessment purposes, you must design one completed costume to be worn in the production and include designs for at least one other costume for the performance. You must also include patterns, preliminary drawings, costings, swatches, materials, and health and safety issues. Your research into the historical background of when *The Crucible* was set will help you with your costume design.

Consider how to produce John Proctor's costume (Photo **B**) for your production of the play. John Proctor's clothes are made to last and must be for working hard in. You may find items of clothing already constructed and adjust them to fit the period of time when the play is set. You must show the type of character he is through your costume design. What accessories would he need? A hat? What type?

B *John Proctor's costume*

C *Abigail Williams' costume*

The Abigail Williams costume will be made from homespun woollen fabric and the strict puritan society in which she lives will be reflected by her clothes. Her hair will be covered in public and all the girls' costumes will reflect these ideals. They will appear like a uniform in some ways.

Summary

You will now have:

- an awareness of the significance and use of costume in a production

- an awareness of the suitability of materials

- a knowledge of the development of design through sketches

- an awareness of other design elements and how they impact on the costume.

Activity

1   Sketch designs for a character in the play. If the character appears in different scenes, consider small changes to the costume – how can you show the character is outdoors, etc.

3.5 Option 8: Make-up

Make-up is the painting of an actor's face to give realistic detail of the face when seen under stage lighting or to create a special character effect.

As a make-up designer creating the make-up for the production of *The Crucible*, you must prepare and present two contrasting stage make-ups. You can make yourself up or make up other members of the cast.

You need to produce diagrams, drawings and notes on usage and costings. You must also consider health and safety issues.

You should experiment with a range of different types of make-up from greasepaint, water-based make-up and crème-based make-up. You also need to consider how the make-up can be successfully removed from your actors. You must always thoroughly clean all materials and brushes at the end of the make-up session.

Your first make-up design could be for Abigail Williams. She is described by Miller as being 'strikingly beautiful' and that will include her skin. A naturalistic make-up is required here.

A *Abigail's naturalistic make-up*

B *John after being tortured*

In contrast to Abigail, to show off your make-up skills appropriately, your next make-up could be for John Proctor at the end of the play after he has been tortured and has spent some considerable weeks in prison. Experiment with wounds and bruises.

Did you know ??????

Traditional stage make-up was called 'greasepaint'. It was a mixture of zinc white, yellow ochre and lard!

3.6   Option 9: Properties

Properties (props) are articles used on stage in the production of a play. There are many opportunities in the script of *The Crucible* for you as a properties designer to produce some valuable work. You must prepare and present two different stage properties for the play. The properties must be manufactured by you. As part of your work in progress, you must produce: a props list for the production as a whole; drawings of the set, indicating where the props are to be sited; and diagrams and notes relating to making, costing and health and safety issues relating to the use of the props.

There a number of ideal situations for the construction of props in *The Crucible*. Let us look to the arrival of Reverend Hale of Beverly during Act One. The stage directions indicate that he arrives loaded down with a large number of books. These could be real books but there would be problems managing to carry large numbers of real books onto the stage. These would be ideal props for you to design and construct, particularly the book needed, which he consults to help him find 'devils'!

Another crucial property needed for *The Crucible* is found in Act Two. Mary Warren returns from the court room, where she has spent all day in the proceedings. During that time she sat sewing and made a poppet for Elizabeth Proctor, her employer. It is described as a 'fair poppet' by Elizabeth when she receives it. Your task would be to create the poppet doll. It is then placed on the fireplace in the room and becomes a vital part of the incriminating evidence used against Elizabeth later in the scene.

A   *A dramatic prop*

kerboodle

3.7 Option 10: Masks

The opportunity to make masks in some plays is limited. However, *The Crucible* offers the mask designer some exciting challenges that can be successfully realised in production terms. By using your imagination and exploration of the themes of *The Crucible*, the task can be successfully completed.

A mask is a covering for the face which is sometimes a disguise or a pretence. It can drastically alter the appearance of the actor wearing it. Your mask research will link you back to the roots of theatre itself in early Greek times, through the Romans, medieval theatre and Shakespearian plays, to the modern day.

Masks can also be used in production terms to stimulate the production itself. Trestle Theatre Company masks confirm this, as their productions are based on the use of their masks to symbolise the emotion that the character is experiencing. This is then used to take the audience through the narrative of the performance. They use their masks as a theatrical tool.

The opening scene of *The Crucible* finds us in the bedroom of Betty Parris as she lies comatose on the bed. She will not speak because she was discovered dancing in the forest by her father and is afraid of her punishment. She was also dabbling in magic! An imaginative way of opening the play would be to re-enact this forest scene. This could include the meeting in the forest of the girls with Tituba. Tituba's origins lie in Barbados, where she was enslaved. Some research into voodoo masks would be appropriate and then the masks could be designed and worn for the spell scene. Some of the older girls in the community could be persuaded to wear masks. Betty would decline and, as a result, would be recognised by her father. Two contrasting masks would then be constructed and worn for assessment purposes.

A *Masks can be simple . . .*

links

www.trestle.org.uk

B *. . . or highly decorated*

Activity

1 a Sketch designs for a character in your play.

  b Discuss them with the actor and costume designer.

Remember

It is important to experiment with your mask design, particularly if the actor wearing the mask has to speak. The mask should also be used in rehearsal.

kerboodle

3.8   Option 11: Puppets

A puppet is a representation of a character. For assessment purposes you must prepare and present a puppet for a play, including drawings, diagrams, methods of construction, considerations of usage and health and safety factors. The puppet must be used in the play.

This option is an exciting challenge to the student who wishes to explore the use of puppetry in *The Crucible*. By exploring some of the storylines running through the play, particularly the opening scene, the puppet designer could rise successfully to the challenge.

The puppet can be representational of a number of styles, including glove puppets, shadow puppets, rod puppets and marionettes.

Your research for this option will open up an interesting world far back in history. For example, Chinese shadow puppets are detailed and sophisticated in both construction and design. You must research the making of these puppets and remember this is a specialist and minority area of study. You must collaborate with the rest of the production team to decide how to integrate puppets into your performance. The scope for this option in *The Crucible* falls at the opening of the play. The forest scene could be imaginatively and successfully represented through shadow puppetry. Careful use of lighting, colour and special effects to include a smoke machine, sound effects and music would produce a spectacular opening to the play.

Although the play opens in the bedroom of Betty Parris, with her father the Reverend Parris praying over her, we are soon aware of the circumstances that have led to Betty being unable to awake. The girls have been dancing in the forest and conjuring spells with Tituba, her nursemaid and slave.

Look at Photo **A**: this scene is from a production by a professional company who often use puppets to tell the narrative of a story. This idea could open your production of *The Crucible*. The figure of the sleeping Betty could feature on stage with your shadow puppets narrating the events that have taken place in the forest.

A   *Horse and Bamboo Theatre Company*

Skills study

Find out about the role of the puppet maker in theatre today.

Activity

1   a   Select a scene where a puppet could be used.

b   Sketch out what the puppet would look like and what it would do.

c   Discuss with the director how it will mesh with the live actors.

Summary

You will have gained:

■ knowledge and use of puppets

■ an understanding of characterisation and use of the puppet in performance

■ an awareness of the puppet's importance to the plot of the play.

3.9 Option 12: Lighting

Lighting is the provision of any source of light to enable the audience to see the action. It also helps to create mood and atmosphere.

Always a popular option, lighting continues to inspire design candidates with ideas for plays studied. For the purposes of this chapter we are looking at *The Crucible*.

In order to be successful you must ensure your lighting rig is adequate for the production needs. Check all health and safety issues in relation to the use and rigging of your lighting design. Is a technician available for these purposes?

You must research colour and design fully and experiment before you begin because poor lighting can ruin the best productions.

You will produce a working lighting plot, rigging diagrams and an annotated script. For purposes of the examination you may only be responsible for lighting a section or scene. Choose your scene carefully. Remember you are working closely with a group of actors and your lights must cover the areas in which they are acting. Beware of shadows and dark areas of the stage.

Explore the use of different types of lanterns and find out what they do. You may even be lucky enough to have 'smart' lights if you have a computerised system. These can certainly add to the 'wow' factor of the production.

The opening of Act Three of *The Crucible* demands that the scene is set in an empty room with sunlight pouring through two high windows in the back wall. The room however is solemn and forbidding. This would be an excellent challenge for any lighting designer, and one that would enable your skills to be successfully assessed.

Study tip

Ensure your lighting is sufficient for all the audience to see the production. Audiences get tired easily if watching performances in semi-darkness for too long.

Key terms

Focus: concentrate the lights onto a specific area of the set.

Angle: the direction from which the light comes onto the set.

Patching: connecting stage lights (lanterns) to dimmer controls for fading in and out.

A   *Opening lighting of the court scene in the RSC production of* **The Crucible**

Summary

You will now have technical understanding of:

- focussing, angling, wiring, operation of the switchboard and dimmer packs and patching.

3.10 Option 13: Sound

As a sound designer for *The Crucible* you must prepare and present a sound plot. Your work must include a practical demonstration of the sound effects necessary for the production. You will need to produce a sound plot, annotated script, diagrams and considerations of health and safety issues.

Sound effects add to the production experience as a whole and are sometimes a vital ingredient in the success of the production. They also add to the production by enhancing and creating mood and atmosphere. The sound effects can be recorded or produced 'live'.

The Crucible offers you a wide range of sound effects necessary for the success of the production.

A *A scene from* **Stomp** *– a piece of musical theatre constructed around sound*

> ### Remember
> Accurate cuing of sound effects is crucial to the success of the production. If, for example, a doorbell sound effect comes after the actor has pressed the bell, a dramatic moment in a production can become one of humour and destroy the atmosphere of the play.

The beginning of Act One gives much scope for experimentation, particularly the section where John Proctor and Abigail Williams are arguing over the 'sleeping' Betty. Reverend Parris has gone downstairs to speak to the congregation to lead them in a psalm, and this is heard coming up from below. The words 'going up to Jesus' are heard, and Betty takes this as her cue to wake up and start screaming. The volume of the psalm is a crucial factor in the successful execution of this scene, and great skill will be required here to add to and build on the tension of the scene. This culminates in the entrance of Rebecca Nurse when 'everything goes quiet'. As a sound technician, you have to decide which sound effects are live and which are recorded. You also have to research the pros and cons of live and recorded sound effects. The direction of the sound effect is also very important – as the stage directions indicate that the sound comes from below, how would you achieve that?

> ### Study tip
> Careful planning and rehearsal of this scene, including the use of the sound effects, is necessary. If the sound effect is too loud the dialogue of the scene will be lost.

3.11 Option 14: Stage management

The production must be managed and run successfully from the first rehearsal to the last performance, and it is the stage manager's role to ensure this is the case.

A *Actors waiting backstage*

This very important role usually develops as your organisational methods and strategies are tested during the rehearsal process. The stage manager must guide the actors and designers to achieve clear understanding of how the performance is managed on stage. You must apply your practical skills by managing the whole performance.

In a large production, the stage manager will be responsible for managing a team of people. This may be the case for you – so you may not only have the actors and designers to manage but a team of assistants too. You need to explore the collaborative nature of the role with the rest of the production team, including the actors. It is your job to tell them what to do. You will also have to demonstrate your knowledge, choice, and use of performance space. You will have to manage entrances and exits successfully and ensure your actors are at the right place at the right time.

B The Crucible, *RSC, Stratford*

As stage manager you are responsible for the overall smooth running of the production. You have responsibility for cueing of lights, changing the set, positioning the props, and this must be carried out with precision and timing.

At the opening of Act Two, the pot must be over the fire and the food ready for John Proctor to eat as he returns from planting the farm. This play offers a great deal of scope for the successful assessment of the stage manager's role. It is also the stage manager's role to stand in for absent colleagues, both in rehearsal and sometimes in performance.

It is a rewarding and challenging role. The role of stage manager requires that you remain calm throughout the rehearsal and performance process. You need to have excellent organisational skills and be authoritative in the way you manage your peers. This part of your role will also gain marks for the way you work as part of the team and you will be assessed by your teacher for your Part 1 mark. Remember too, when everyone else has taken the applause, you have to set everything ready for the smooth running of the next performance.

The stage manager's role is challenging but fun. You will need to supervise some of the rehearsals and even take some group rehearsals yourself. You will be the director's greatest friend and you will work in close harmony with all the production team as you manage them towards and including the performance.

Summary

You will have gained:

■ an understanding of the responsibility of the stage manager's role before, during and after the production.

The work you do on this Controlled Assessment task will be useful in all elements of this course. Your practical skills will be relevant to all other practical tasks and you will be able to analyse them and write about them on the written paper.

Unit 1: The written paper

The Controlled Assessment task is ideal for answering questions in Section A or Section B.

For Section A, you will be asked to answer four questions and you will describe, explain, analyse and evaluate the practical work you completed during the course.

The work you have produced on *The Crucible* will be an excellent choice, as your answer will take the examiner through the exciting process you experienced as you put the play together for performance. You may answer this section on any Controlled Assessment Option you have completed during the course. You may focus your answer as an actor, designer or technician.

You can see that it is therefore very important to keep a record of the work you have done. You may keep a diary, with a series of recordings or photographs. You could make videos of rehearsals,

which will also help you to refine your work. Make sure that you have a video of your final performance, as this will help you revise for the written paper.

Design and technical students will have a detailed record of their progress as part of their practical assessment, and this will be an excellent revision tool too.

This question carries 40 marks, half of the marks for the whole paper. You will have to revise the work thoroughly so that you can give plenty of detail. You will be able to use clearly labelled sketches and diagrams in your answer, so practice these in your revision period.

In Section B, you will be asked to answer questions on the study and performance of a scripted play. You will describe how you communicated your character, design or technical skill to an audience and will evaluate the success in performance.

You will have 45 minutes to write your answer.

Unit 2: The Controlled Assessment task

When you have finished your work on *The Crucible*, you will perform it in front of an audience. This could be the rest of your group, friends and relatives, a school assembly or the public. A moderator may be present and their job is to moderate the marking of your teacher.

Your teacher will award you a mark for your preparation, so his or her feedback will be very important. You should show an awareness of how you can develop your work and you should be able to work co-operatively and creatively in the group.

Whether you have chosen a design option or a performance option, your teacher will be looking for evidence that you can:

- discuss your knowledge and understanding of work in progress
- generate, explore and develop ideas during the process of development
- recognise your strengths and weaknesses both in the process of working towards a performance and in performance
- demonstrate an understanding of your own capabilities and the demands of working in a group
- discuss and assess your performance.

In your final performance you will be assessed on how you use your practical skills to put your ideas across to the audience. Your practical skills will be assessed, whether you offer acting, design or technical work, and they are all of equal value to the end product.

Whether you have chosen a design option or a performance option, your teacher and moderator will be looking for evidence that you can:

- interpret a play with creativity and originality
- show an awareness of the audience
- use practical skills to communicate with clarity, fluency, control and appropriateness
- consider relevant health and safety factors.

The most important thing to remember is to enjoy this experience. You will have rehearsed for weeks and planned carefully for success, now go out and achieve it.

4 Improvisation

In this chapter you will learn to:

work with others to create characters

think quickly and develop your ideas

accept ideas from others and develop them

respond positively – say 'yes and …' – to develop the ideas of others in the group

share decision-making and listen to others.

Study tip

When you are improvising, keep notes after each session and record targets for the next session. It is also useful to video work in progress.

If you were going to the theatre to see an improvised play, what would you expect to see? Would it be a series of funny quick-fire sketches or a play which was being made up on the spot? In fact, you would not be able to tell whether the starting point of the production was a script or a series of improvisations. By the time the play is performed in front of the audience, it will have been designed, costumed, lit and fully rehearsed.

You can use improvisational skills to:

- develop a play
- make up scenes or characters on a theme to use in devised work
- develop an understanding of a character in a text you are working on
- develop an understanding of the relationships between characters in a play you are working on
- try out scenes in a play you are going to see
- try out technical and design ideas.

If you choose the Controlled Assessment, Option 3: Improvisation, you will be able to make an improvised play. You may start with a given stimulus which may be to create and develop a character and then, in a group, you can structure your material so that it will engage and interest your audience. You will also have the opportunity to make decisions about stage form, setting, costume and all other design and technical elements. When your play is fully rehearsed, it will be ready to present to your audience.

The renowned film and theatre director Mike Leigh has created many improvised plays, such as *Nuts in May*, *Abigail's Party* and most recently *Two Thousand Years*. He begins by working with a team of actors who each create and develop a character. He then sets up scenes and selects the material he wants to include in his final play. This is a long and detailed process.

A Two Thousand Years, *National Theatre*

Getting started

Starter activity

With a partner, try this series of short improvisations:

- a meeting between a parent and a teacher about a difficult student
- a young person explaining to a parent that they are leaving home
- an estate agent giving details to a client of a property that the agency is desperate to sell
- a business executive complaining about a late train to a member of the station staff.

When you have tried out these short **improvisations**, decide who you think is 'in charge' in each scene. It may not be the obvious person.

Now pick one improvisation from those you have just tried. Try it again but, this time, put emphasis on the **status** of the character you think is 'least in charge'. Your aim is to raise their status. You can do this by thinking about your body language, gestures and how you use your voice. And, of course, what you say will have a bearing on the status of the character.

You can try a whole series of changes to develop the improvisation. For example, you could change the age of the characters or alter the mood of one character as the improvisation progresses.

Activity

1 Choose the scene which you think is working well in showing the characters and **structure** it by deciding on your starting point, what set you will have on stage and what props you could use. Rehearse the scene and present your short piece of polished improvisation to your audience. Use the audience feedback when you evaluate your work for Unit 2.

Study tip

You will need to refer to movement, gesture and vocal skills when you are analysing your work in Unit 1, the written paper, and also when you are evaluating your work in Unit 2, the practical work.

Remember

You and your partner do not both need to be on stage all the time.

Key terms

Improvisation: a method that actors use to create, develop and communicate characters and situations so that they can make up a play; in GCSE Drama, improvisation refers to any unscripted work.

Status: which character is the most or least powerful in the scene; power isn't shown by shouting or towering over someone.

Structure: organising your work, in terms of its starting point, its setting and any props that are available

kerboodle

4.1 Creating a character

All types of drama need characters, and improvised work is no exception. In scripted work you can rely on the playwright for the script, characters and theme, but in improvised work you must rely on your experience, imagination and research.

There are many different **stimuli** which can be used to create characters, but a useful starting point is to think of someone you know. Choose someone who is old than you and of the same sex – it's hard enough developing a character without having to act a different gender as well. Choose someone who is not known to other people in your drama group or your school. You need not know the person very well because you will use your imagination to build up details that you do not or could never know about them.

Building a physical picture

Try these individual exercises.

Activities

1. Imagine that you (as your character) are waiting:
   - in a doctor's waiting room
   - at a bus stop
   - outside the boss's office.

2. Try to get a sense of how your character would feel and what they would look like in each situation.

3. Show how they would stand, any gestures they might use and anything they might have with them. There is no need to do anything 'dramatic'. The point is just to think about their physicality. You will be able to think of many more ideas.

4. Now think about what your character's kitchen would be like and, in role, make a hot drink. Think all the time about what they would do, and **mime** the whole sequence.

   All the time you are working, show in as detailed a way as possible about how you are doing everything: how you fill the kettle, open the cupboards and wait for the kettle to boil. Build up a picture in your mind of the style of kitchen, the type of hot drink being prepared and the general tidiness of the kitchen.

Key terms

Stimulus (plural stimuli): the starting-point for a devised work; the idea, image or object that sparks off your work.

Mime: using clear gestures and movements but no words to convey a character's personality and emotions.

Extension activity

1. Imagine that your character is going out for the evening. Mime opening their wardrobe and looking through and selecting the clothes they might wear.

2. This will give you the chance to think about their personal appearance. Do they spend lots of money on their clothes or are they creative on a small budget? Are there particular styles they favour? What about colour and fabrics? Are fashion trends important? Would they dress up for a night out with friends or not bother?

Building a vocal picture

Try out different ideas to help you think about the voice of your character. Again, imagine your character in various situations where you can get a sense of the different tones of voice and the language they would use. Remember that everyone has particular ways of speaking which are appropriate at different times. We use different language with our friends than we would use, for example, at work. In formal situations our choice of vocabulary is appropriate to the situation we find ourselves in and, if we are trying to persuade someone to do something for us, then not only our language but also our **tone** and **pace** changes.

Key terms

Tone: using your voice to express what you are feeling.

Pace: the speed and rhythm of your speech and how you pick up cues from others.

Activity

5   Still working alone, use the idea of telephone calls to experiment with the voice of your character. Practise your character trying to make a call to:

- persuade someone to give you a lift
- make an excuse
- make a complaint
- arrange to meet someone.

How does your character's voice change in each scene?

Study tip

Make brief notes about the voice, movements, facial expressions and gestures of your character. These are all points you will later analyse when answering Unit 1 written examination questions, and evaluating your work for Unit 2.

A   *Imagination and conviction will aid making your characters believable*

Already the character you are creating will have moved away from the real person you started with and your imagination will be filling in the gaps.

B   **The Grizzled Skipper** *written by Maggie Nevill*

Once you have got the basics of your character, you will need to develop the role into a believable character who you can put into a play. One of the most straightforward ways of doing this is to work in small groups of four people and to **hot-seat** each character in turn.

You must answer the questions put to you **as the character** because this will give you further practice in sitting, speaking and moving as him or her. Now is a good time to invent a name for your character, but avoid choosing one that is too close to the name of the person you first started with.

There are hundreds of questions you could be asked and you will have to be quick-thinking and answer straight away, inventing answers and therefore details of your character.

The questions put to you will be basic to start with, asking things such as name, age, marital status and employment status. Inquisitive members of your group will then move on to ask about what sort of car you drive or what sort of house you live in so that they can work out how much money you have. You may then be asked about what is important in your life so that they can find out about your beliefs and your personal relationships.

A *Two actors rehearsing* **The Cage**, *written by Deborah Gearing, Nuffield Theatre*

> ### Key terms
>
> **Hot-seating**: the technique of an actor staying in role while answering questions from the audience about the character's thoughts and feelings.

> ### Activity
>
> **1** Give a scenario (an event, initial sentence or scene) to two characters and see how they develop it.

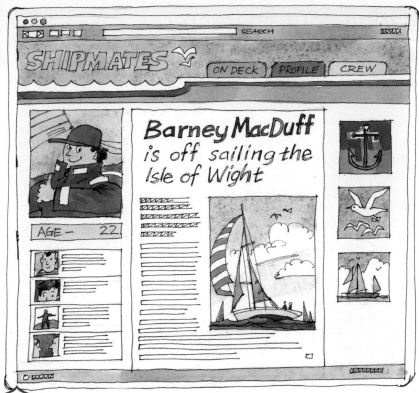

B *Using online aids such as social networking sites can help in visualising new characters*

Remember, you should keep notes throughout the development process. They may be useful for when you are constructing your play and will be essential for when you are performing. You could record your notes in diary form, showing how you have progressed from each practical session. Alternatively, you could make a poster of a profile page for a social networking site that includes basic factual details about your employment, status, interests and friends. This will help to build up ideas of your character and their relationships with others. You could add a photo of yourself looking like the character or draw a picture or choose a photo from a newspaper or magazine but avoid choosing anyone recognisable or famous.

Activity

2 To further develop your character, try this exercise.

a **Work with a partner**

One of you will play the part of your character and the other will be in role as the parent.

- The scene is at home, and the time is 6.00pm
- The parent is at home and the character enters
- You have some very good news to tell.
- Set the scene and run the improvisation.

You will find out what actually is good news for your character and how s/he behaves in this situation. You may also be able to use the content in your play. (Remember what is good news for you may not be for the parent)

Now you can swap over.

b Now try different variations. You could tell:

- bad news to a friend
- gossip to a work colleague
- a secret to a sibling
- a lie to your boss

You will be able to think of many different variations to suit the character you are playing.

Communicating your character to an audience

You need to see if your character can be performed and appreciated by an audience, so you will need to develop, rehearse and perform a short piece.

Work by yourself and prepare a **monologue** to perform. You could write it and learn it if you wish. Assume that it is a speech which will be the opening moment of a play and, as you will be on stage alone, you could imagine you were making a phone call or answering a call. You could be recording a video diary or talking directly to the audience.

All drama needs **conflict,** and so in your speech show that you are struggling with something in your life. For example, it may be a relationship problem or it may be a decision you have to make.

In this version of a speech from *Twelfth Night* Viola, alone on stage, has realised that Olivia has been taken in by her disguise, believes her to be a man and has fallen in love with her.

VIOLA   **I left no ring with her. What means this lady?**
Fortune forbid my outside have not charmed her.
She made good view of me... indeed, so much,
That sure methought her eyes had lost her tongue...
[For she did speak in starts distractedly.
She loves me, sure. The cunning of her passion
Invites me in this churlish messenger.
None of my lord's ring? Why, he sent her none.]
I am the man. If it be so, as 'tis,
Poor lady, she were better love a dream.
[Disguise, I see thou art a wickedness
Wherein the pregnant enemy does much.
How easy is it for the proper-false
In women's waxen hearts to set their forms!
Alas, our frailty is the cause, not we,
For such as we are made of, such we be.
How will this fadge? My master loves her dearly;
And I, poor monster, fond as much on him;
And she, mistaken, seems to dote on me.]
What will become of this? As I am man,
My state is desperate for my master's love;
As I am woman – now alas the day –
What thriftless sighs shall poor Olivia breathe?
O Time, thou must untangle this, not I.
It is too hard a knot for me to untie.

A   *Viola and Olivia from* **Twelfth Night**

Twelfth Night, by William Shakespeare, from **The Cut Shakespeare**, *by Steve Gooch*

When you perform your work, if possible, use costume, props and lighting to give a sense of place and time. Decide what mood you want to put across and use movements, gestures and voice so that the audience gets the message.

The following extract is one of a series of short monologues from *A Memory of Lizzie,* where Eliza or Edward, followed by others, is giving evidence. Although s/he is not alone on stage, notice how the stage directions make it seem as though s/he is, by isolating her.

You could try performing this. Work with a partner as a director and use your movement, gesture and voice to show how horrified Eliza or Edward are.

(Main stage lights dim, spotlight on Eliza. The rest of the cast is in the shadows.)

Eliza: 'I went into the sitting room and saw the form of Mr Borden lying on the sofa. His face was very badly cut with apparently a sharp object. There was blood all over his face; his face was covered in blood. I felt his pulse and satisfied myself he was dead, and took a glance about the room and saw that nothing was disturbed at all. The body was lying with its face to the right side, apparently at ease, as anyone would if they were asleep. I could hardly recognise the face.'

(Stage lights back up, spotlight out. Break the freeze slowly.)

As well as performing your own monologue, you will also be a member of the audience for the other actors in your group. When you are watching you should make notes on what the actor did. Keep your notes simple but be precise. Write down how the performance made you feel and what the actor did to achieve that effect. It may be that they spoke slowly and used a low tone to show their sadness, or that they sat slumped in their chair. They may have entered slowly, dragging their feet. On the other hand, they may have run in laughing as they did so and showed how excited they were by fidgeting with their hair.

B The Cage *by Deborah Gearing. What can you tell about this boy from what he is doing?*

4.4 Making your play

When you start to put ideas together for your play, you will need to be flexible and creative. When your group comes together you will all have lots of information about your own character and that of others. A theme or storyline may have begun to suggest itself to you, or you may have been inspired by some preparatory work you have done.

If you have worked on monologues you may have found one really interesting and you may want to use it in your performance. If so, it may become the starting point for your work, or it might be the conclusion. You could use it as the cue for a **flashback** moment.

You may need to make some adjustments to your characterisation so that you and your group can develop ideas about how all the characters can come together in one piece of work. You may, for example, need to make your character much older, but it will be interesting to try out improvisations with your character at different moments in their lives.

You may decide to make all the characters much older than at first.

Activity

1 Try improvising the following situations:

- at a school reunion, looking back at your younger days and showing how well you've done
- being interviewed for a promotion at work, perhaps by someone you used to know
- at a retirement party, looking forward or maybe back.

In your play, make sure that each actor has a specific and different role so that you do not end up with characters with the same point of view as this can lead to repetitive work. Make sure that your storyline is clear and that all members of the group have the opportunity to show their skills. Be sure about the journey each character will take and any conflict within or between the characters.

It's a good idea now to write a **scenario** so that you get an idea of the narrative and also of the shape of the work. You can use a variety of scenes so that the audience will remain interested throughout. You can keep a list or make a series of sketches or photographs to keep track of what's happening.

You will need to make some decisions about the period that your work takes place in. You have probably set it in modern times but there may be scope for varying this. This decision will have implications for costume and set design.

A *What can you note about this production of* **Abigail's Party** *by Mike Leigh and directed by David Gridley? Look at costume, hair styles, props and settings*

Decide also about the **style** and **genre**, and be consistent throughout the piece.

Be sure also about the location for the play. While you are rehearsing bear in mind that changes in location are going to be tricky to put on stage; and you will want to avoid a stop–start structure as this will lose the attention of the audience.

As you rehearse, keep track of the changes that you make so that you do not waste time going back over old ground. It's a good idea, at the end of each practical session, to decide which part you will rehearse next time. This will avoid the problem of always starting at the beginning so that part of the work is excellent but the excellence is not sustained through the whole play. Also make sure that everyone is busy in each rehearsal. If one person is not acting they should be sitting where the audience will be and making notes about how the work is looking from the audience's point of view.

Key terms

Style: how the play is performed, such as in a naturalistic fashion or physically.

Genre: the type of production, for example comedy, tragedy, thriller or documentary.

Remember

Avoid the need for blackouts and messy scene changes.

B *Director Katie Henry from the Orange Tree Theatre Company giving notes in rehearsal*

4.5 Rehearsing and performing

Now that your play is set and no further changes will take place, you can concentrate on the performance of your role.

While you are rehearsing you will be refining your performance skills and working on your movement, gesture and voice and, of course, on how you will react to other characters on stage. The way you use your acting skills will make it clear how you feel about the other characters as well as what you actually say. Check the following:

■ Are you using vocabulary appropriate to your role? (This may mean that you will have to do some research, especially if the character does a job that you are not familiar with.)

■ Is your accent appropriate? (If you are playing someone older than you, avoid using slang expressions.)

■ Is your tone of voice different when speaking to different characters?

  ▪ Does your physicality show:
  ▪ whether the person you are speaking to is superior or inferior to you?
  ▪ whether you like them or not?
  ▪ whether you want them to do something for you?
  ▪ whether you are afraid of them or they are afraid of you?

As you approach the technical rehearsal make decisions about set, costume, props, lighting and any other technical devices. If you are lucky enough to have technical students in your group, you will have worked on these all the way through your rehearsal period but if not you will have to organise this yourselves. At the technical rehearsal, you should go through your play from **cue to cue** and finalise all set, costume and lighting changes. Don't worry about the acting apart from the entrances and exits.

Once this is set and recorded you will be ready for your **dress rehearsal**. This should be as close to the actual performance as possible. Try to have an audience, and pay attention to their feedback. Simple points can be very helpful, such as whether they can hear you and whether they can actually understand what is happening, as well as more detailed information about what they noticed about your acting skills.

If you are thoroughly prepared you will really enjoy your performance, and so will your audience.

A   **Abigail's Party** *by Mike Leigh and directed by David Gridley. Take note of the set design, the colours and scheme of props*

■ Recording your achievements

You have created and developed a character, put your character into a group and selected and shaped your ideas to produce a piece of rehearsed improvisation which you have performed to an audience. You have had feedback from an audience and provided feedback to others. You have used performance and technical skills to communicate your ideas to an audience.

It is essential to keep notes of all this. You could use a series of photos or a diary of how you created the work. Everyone in the group should have copies of this and your work must be recorded and retained as evidence of your achievement. You should also record an evaluation of your work

You may complete this Controlled Assessment task long before the final exam, and this record will be an ideal piece of work to use when you are answering Section A on Unit 1.

> **Remember**
>
> The audience should not know whether this is a scripted or an improvised play.

4.6 Option 6: Set design

If you choose set design as your Unit 2 assessment option, you will be working as part of a group and while the actors are developing their roles and making their play you will need to take careful note of how the work is progressing and who the characters are.

You will need to come up with ideas for the location of the play and how it is going to look on stage. You will be able to influence the outcome of the work if you can suggest imaginative ideas about the stage form which you think will be most effective and how to express the mood of the play.

As the work develops

- Make a scale **ground plan** of your performance space. Use the scale 1:25 and mark on it all permanent features such as doors and the lighting rig. (Make lots of copies.)
- Sketch on the plan how different types of stage would work and where the audience would be.
- Collect materials you will need for your model.
- Begin to collect and research sources for the actual set.
- Begin to sketch ideas with samples of colours, materials and texture.

Objectives

In this unit you will learn to:

work as part of a group

research the period

sketch ideas

make a ground plan

work to scale

make a model

construct the set.

Key terms

Ground plan: a scale outline of the set drawn as if from above with indications of flats and furniture marked on it.

A *Designer's model of the set for* **Abigail's Party** *by Mike Leigh, directed by David Gridley*

During rehearsals

Take careful notes of the rehearsals so that you can be clear about the mood of the play and the location that the set needs to communicate to the audience.

It is likely that in improvised work a naturalistic piece will be created, so you may need to collect furniture which gives a sense of how at least one of the characters lives.

Present your ideas to the group and remember to consult with any other members of the group who are also working on a design skill. Try to accommodate the actors' needs in your design but also try to avoid a series of short scenes and suggest solutions to keep the play flowing, such as a **composite set**.

Any furniture you include in your set design must be suited to the character whose home you are showing and to the period in which the play is set. If you are using flats to suggest walls they must be painted or papered appropriately, and make sure that you discuss your colour scheme with the actor and with the person responsible for costumes. There will be some items which are needed because of the plot but be sure to dress your set appropriately too.

Health and safety is very important for the set designer. So consider:

- fire precautions, fireproofing and fire exits
- backstage safety for the actors
- front of house safety for your audiences.

You should be completely ready for the technical rehearsal.

The photograph opposite shows how detailed the designers model should be. The play is set in the 1970s and fully reflects the period and the taste of Beverley whose home it is. Note the leather furniture, the well-stocked cocktail cabinet, the ornaments and pictures which dress the set and the wallpaper and colour scheme.

Study tip

It would be very useful if, during the hot-seating sessions, you could ask questions, which will encourage the actors to think about their environment and how they think they might furnish their home.

Key terms

Composite set: a set on which it is possible to perform scenes in different locations without having to change the set all the time. *Blue Remembered Hills*, for example, needs a composite set to keep the action moving.

Remember

The set is often the first thing that the audience sees as they enter the theatre, so giving as much information as you can about the play is vitally important and this should be sending the right messages about the play.

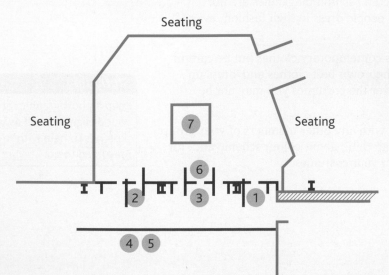

Unit list:
1) S/R Single door
2) S/L Double door
3) S/C Double door
4) CYC Flats
5) CYC Jacks
6) False procenium
7) Centre platform

Sketch of ground plan

4.7 Option 7: Costume design

When we meet someone for the first time, we make an immediate judgement about them (whether we should do or not) and this is based on what they look like and what clothes they are wearing. Look around at the people in your drama group. Even if you are all wearing school uniform you will all be wearing it in your own way and showing hints of your own personality. Out of school, in real life, as soon as you start making your own decisions about what you will wear, your clothes say something about you: this is also true of characters on stage. Your costume design will be giving the audience clues about the characters they see and will also help the actors to feel more like the characters they are playing.

■ As the work develops

- Make a list of the characters and the sorts of people they are.
- Join in the hot-seating and ask detailed questions about the clothes they might like.
- Note if anyone needs particular accessories.
- Note if anyone needs a special costume, such as a secret pocket.
- Make notes about the relationships between the characters as the colour or style you use may give clues about it to the audience.

■ During rehearsals

You will be able to decide which costume you would like to make or assemble and which you would like to provide sketches for. When you are putting your ideas together use dress pattern catalogues and/or mail order catalogues, or find out from the actor which shops they think their characters would go to. Try going into stores or departments you wouldn't usually shop in especially if you are designing for an older character. Fashion magazines are not particularly helpful as not many people dress in high fashion, even if they'd like to.

Improvised drama often requires contemporary clothes but be careful of actors who want to bring in their own best clothes and 'dress up'. Try to keep some control even over the costumes you may not be designing for.

Remember to discuss your work with any other members of your group working on design so that you can think about colour scheme and, for example, the effect of lighting on your costumes.

Objectives

In this section you will learn to:

work as part of a group

research the period

sketch ideas

discuss the characters with the actors

research fabrics, textures and colour

keep careful notes or illustrations as your ideas develop.

Study tip

Keep a photographic record of your designs as well as your sketches to help with revision you may need to do.

A   *Production of* **Billy Liar** *in 1960*

Look at Photo **A** and notice how the designer has put the characters and period across.

In the photograph above you will see Billy Fisher and his Dad.

- Dad is wearing a sleeveless knitted pullover and a neat shirt and tie
- His spectacles are in period and yet help show his overbearing attitude
- Billy has not got dressed yet. He is wearing boyish stripped pjamas
- As a dressing gown he is wearing an old mac, showing a casual attitude
- He is having a fantasy moment, hence the coin in his eye as a monocle.

You should be completely ready for the technical rehearsal.

Remember

- Don't forget practical details such as making sure that there is time for measuring and fitting your costume, budgeting and shopping for fabric.
- Collect accessories and be willing to help with hairstyles and make-up.
- Take note of health and safety matters; make sure that the costumes are fireproof and that they are comfortable for the actors to wear.

4.8 Option 8: Make-up

If you choose to specialise in make-up, you will need to prepare and present two contrasting make-ups. In improvised work, the actors often create naturalistic characters, so you will have to perfect your skills of creating straight or character make-up.

As the work develops

- Keep notes on all the characters as they develop.
- Look out for any opportunities for the use of make-up.
- Get your make-up kit in order.
- Research the types of make-up you will need.
- Try to find time to practise on a couple of people in the group.

During rehearsals

Choose the people you will want to make up. As you need contrasting characters, choose an older character and perhaps you'll be lucky and have someone who needs a scar, a wound or a beard.

Decide whether you are going to use greasepaint, in which case you will need sticks for foundation and liners. You will also need powder to set the make-up, and removal cream. If you use cake foundation you will need to apply it with your fingertips or a sponge, and if you use a cream foundation you will also need powder.

If you are working in a small performance space you will need to be subtle in your application. Check your make-up under the appropriate lighting. When you are ageing a character think about how their skin tone will change and look for the natural places on their face to see where their wrinkles will develop. Remember that wrinkles are not lines but little furrows, so will need to be shaded and highlighted to create the effect. A product called Wrinkle Stipple is a light latex, which may be useful.

If you are making a beard or moustache, choose crepe hair of the appropriate colour and be sure to use spirit gum and the appropriate remover.

You should be completely ready for the technical rehearsal.

Objectives

In this section you will learn to:

work as part of a group

research types of make-up

sketch ideas

discuss the characters with the actors

keep careful notes or illustrations as your ideas develop.

∞ links

www.backstageshop.co.uk/acatalog/Leichner.html

www.stagemakeuponline/bennye

Study tip

Health and safety are very important. Be sure that everything is perfectly clean before and after use. Make sure you are aware of any allergies an actor may have.

A *Make-up applied pre-performance*

4.9 Option 9: Properties

As you get to know the characters and the play, you will be able to make a full list of the props needed in the production and it would be a good plan to come up with ideas of your own so that you can show your abilities as well as possible. You will need to make two props. Try writing a props list for the photo on page 71.

As the work develops

- When you have got your full list, make a list of when they appear on stage.
- If they are personal props, list who they belong to.
- Research how you will get hold of them.
- Will you have to hire anything?
- Which props will you make?
- Start sketching your ideas in terms of style and construction.

During rehearsals

Be prepared to be flexible but let everyone know what you are making so that you do not have to change your plans. Consult with the set designer, if there is one, and with the rest of the group.

Make sure your props are safe and are completely ready by the technical rehearsal.

> **Objectives**
>
> In this section you will learn to:
>
> work as part of a group
>
> be aware of the use of properties and how they can enhance the work
>
> research the period and style that the work is set in
>
> sketch ideas
>
> experiment with materials
>
> make props which will stand up to the rigours of performance.

> **Study tip**
>
> Make sure the props you choose show your skills. For example, you might decide on a piece of intricate jewellery or a false hand. Whatever it is, keep careful notes of your progress and photograph your results.

A *In this scene from* **Old King Cole** *by Ken Campbell, the prop maker constructed both the ton weight and the washing machine which an actor had to climb into. Both had to be very sturdy*

4.10 Option 10: Masks

Masks are very important in the history of drama; they go back to the Greeks and the beginning of drama. If you are designing and making masks for a piece of improvised work you will have to come up with your own ideas and take part in the development of the work in order to give yourself creative opportunities.

■ As the work develops

- Get to know the characters very well so that you can make suggestions about how they could use masks.
- Be involved in the development of the storyline.
- Organise your materials and make sketches and diagrams.
- Consult with the actors and the costume designer.

■ During rehearsals

Look out for opportunities such as having the characters attend a fancy dress ball, using hand-held masks which reveal their true personalities or using half-masks when there has to be a quick character change.

Decide on which type of mask will be appropriate and make your mask simply using a sticky brown paper base which you can build up on the actor's face. This will mean that it fits them exactly. When the base is finished you can add natural or exaggerated features and then paint it appropriately. This can be cut down to use as a half-mask or used full-face.

If an actor is using a mask they need to be aware of how to present a mask to the audience so you should watch rehearsals carefully to make sure the mask can be seen. Give yourself plenty of time to make the mask and give the actor plenty of time to rehearse in it. Be very careful about health and safety. Keep everything clean and make sure that the mask fits the actor properly, is comfortable and that they can see through it. It must be strong enough to last through all performances.

You should be completely ready by the technical rehearsal.

A *Masks used in an interesting way*

Study tip

If you are making more than one mask, then be sure to label them correctly.

4.11   Option 11: Puppets

There are many different types of puppets, from marionettes to shadow and glove puppets, and all are representational rather than naturalistic, so you will have to suggest ways in which a puppet could contribute to the group work.

As the work develops

- Watch the work and pay attention to how the plot is developing.
- Gather your research and make notes and sketches.
- Decide on the type of puppet you would like to design and construct.
- Gather materials and begin to experiment with ideas.
- Begin your designs.

During rehearsals

Suggest how the puppet could help the development and performance of the work. Your puppet could represent a child of one of the characters or the character as a child, and scenes could be built around it. It could represent the conscience of a character and appear in a scene where the character is struggling with his or her inner thoughts. This would be a useful exercise to do for all the characters.

The puppet could help to show part of the story which can't be acted on stage, such as a chase or someone travelling a long distance. However you decide to use your puppet you must also manipulate it. What will you wear when you are doing this?

If you are making a glove puppet, make sure that its costume is large enough to allow flexible movement and make sure that you have plenty of rehearsal time.

If you decide to use shadow puppets, you will need to construct the screen and experiment with the light behind it to create the required effect.

You should be completely ready by the technical rehearsal.

A A medieval glove-puppet booth c.1340

kerboodle

4.12 Option 12: Lighting

As the work develops

As a lighting designer, you need to make sure that the actors can be seen, as well as contribute to the overall feeling of the work by lighting appropriately in terms of focus, intensity and colour. You will also be able to help with the flow and continuity of the work by using cross-fades instead of blackouts to move the action on and to change the mood of the work scene by scene.

- You will need to watch and make notes on the development of the characters.
- Keep notes of the location(s) being suggested.
- Discuss your ideas with the group and suggest how the lighting will help.
- Get to know your equipment and make sure it is all in working order.
- If the actors are presenting short pieces, light them.
- Experiment with lighting actors' faces without shadows.

During rehearsals

Decide on the stage form (see page 46) and what the set will look like, and begin to set it out in your drama space. Keep really detailed notes and diagrams. It is a good idea to tape the position of your set on the floor of your drama space as you do not want to have to re-rig your **lanterns** if furniture etc. is in the wrong place. You will need a very detailed scenario as there will not be an actual script for this work.

Experiment with the effects you can create. Try out different coloured **gels** and note the effect on set and costume. Use **gobos** to see if you can create different locations and try focusing spotlights or using barn doors to create small lit areas.

You must keep records of everything you do so that you can write an accurate cue sheet which should have numbered cues, channels, levels and timings. It should be clear enough for someone else to operate it if necessary.

You should be completely ready for the technical rehearsal where you will have the chance to adjust and develop your design and the timing of each cue.

(see page 46)

Show:				Date:	Op:
Page no.	Cue no.	In time	Out time	Description of cue	Action on stage

A *An example of a lighting cue sheet*

Objectives

In this section you will learn to:

work as part of a group

understand how lanterns, the lighting board and the dimmer pack works

rig and focus

operate from a cue sheet.

Key terms

Lanterns: lights used to illuminate a set.

Lighting board: a control desk for lighting.

Dimmer pack: a number of dimmer controls mounted in a cabinet.

Rig: hang the lanterns in the correct positions.

Focus: concentrate the lights onto a specific area of the set.

Cue sheet: a list of the lighting changes throughout the production.

Gel: a coloured film placed in front of a lantern to change the colour of the light on stage (also known as a colour filter).

Gobo: a small metal plate inserted behind a spotlight to project an image onto the stage.

Study tip

If other groups are working in the same space, use a different colour of tape for each group when you are marking out your set.

kerboodle

4.13 Option 13: Sound

As a sound designer, you will need to be aware of the needs of the play but also to suggest your own ideas about how you can indicate the moods of different scenes or sections. You may be asked for specific sound effects, such as a chiming clock, but you also need to be aware of how else you can use your skills to contribute to the overall effect.

As the work develops

- Join in the hot-seating sessions and find out about the musical tastes of the characters.
- Keep a track of the action and anticipate effects you might need.
- Listen to lots of music and record some which might be useful.
- Research sound-effects CDs.
- Experiment by comparing pre-recorded sounds with those you can use live – which are most successful?
- Make suggestions about music to begin and end the play.
- Try your sounds through speakers both backstage and front-of-house.

During rehearsals

Make sure that you have an up-to-date scenario and note where the sound will be needed. If you need to record any of the actors, give yourself plenty of time and be prepared so that they know what is expected of them. Make sure that you have clear notes about the order in which they are needed so that you will be able to make a detailed **cue sheet**. Your cue sheet should have numbered cues and should show when the cue happens – it may be with the lighting, on an entrance of a character or a line spoken. It should also show how it fades in and out, how many seconds it will last how loud it is and which speakers will be used.

You should be completely ready by the technical rehearsal, when you will be able to finalise your cues: their placing, length and volume.

Objectives

In this section you will learn to:

work as part of a group

assess what equipment you are able to use

make sure you know everything works

check that the speakers are moveable

keep details of the character and plot.

Show:				Date:			Op:	
Page no.	Cue no.	Device	Disc name	Track no.	Track name	Track length	Track description	Action on stage

A *An example of a sound cue sheet*

Study tip

Always try to fade effects and music in and out, unless it's something like a gunshot.

4.14 Option 14: Stage management

The stage manager is the linchpin of a successful show. If you are stage-managing an improvised piece you will be meticulous in your record-keeping. You will be able to save the group lots of time if you record what happens in each rehearsal and set targets for what you will be doing in the next session. You will work closely with the director throughout.

■ As the work develops

- Make careful notes.
- Join in the hot-seating and keep details of the characters as they develop.
- Begin to make notes of where the action will happen.
- Start to collect props and furniture for rehearsals.
- Organise the writing of a scenario.
- Use the scenario to begin your **prompt copy**.
- Keep notes of changes as you go along.
- As the play is still 'in progress', be flexible.
- Discuss what **stage form** you are going to use.
- Note any health and safety implications for the actors or the audience.
- Deal with the rest of the group sensitively.

■ During rehearsals

When the work is at the stage where it can be rehearsed you will need to make decisions about set and costumes. If you have other design colleagues consult with them.

Tape the set out onto the floor of your performance space so that rehearsals can be organised and lighting can be fixed. Work out where you will be during the performances so that you can easily communicate with the sound and lighting operators. You will need to collect props and costumes and work out where they will be stored. Keep these secure as lots of time can be wasted searching for a missing item. It sounds mean, but do not lend your props to other groups. Keep records of where the props will come on and off stage. Check where costumes will be if a quick change is needed.

By now you should know if you will have to hire or borrow anything. Members of staff in your school or college are good sources, but it is a good idea to check out hire opportunities in your area and keep a list of phone numbers. You may have to go out 'propping' or shopping, so be sure of your budget.

Objectives

In this section you will learn to:

work as part of a group

organise the group rehearsals

communicate with technical and design team members

run the technical and dress rehearsals

keep your prompt copy up to date

run the show.

Key terms

Prompt copy: a very detailed copy of the details of the performance with all cues (acting and technical) marked on it.

Stage form: the arrangement of the acting area and audience in your performance space.

A The Orange Tree Theatre Company rehearse

There should be enough room backstage to keep your props table, for efficient exits and entrances and for health and safety purposes. All wires must be taped down securely and scenery firmly fixed. Be very tidy and hope that the rest of the group will follow your example.

Making your prompt copy

You will have a very detailed scenario by now.

Write the details of each scene on one page and face this with a blank sheet. If any of the work has been scripted include the script.

Write on the blank sheet the exits and entrances and where the actors are on the stage.

Divide your acting area and use the abbreviations shown in Figure A. The positions on stage are from the actors' point of view.

Upstage right (USR)	Upstage centre (USC)	Upstage left (USL)
Centre right (CR)	Centre stage (C)	Centre left (CL)
Downstage right (DSR)	Downstage centre (DSC)	Downstage left (DSL)

Audience

B *These are the abbreviations for the different areas of the stage*

Key terms

Standby cue: a warning to the operator to be ready for a change in lighting or sound.

Go cue: an instruction to the operator to carry out a change in lighting or sound.

On the blank page, write all your cues and note in the script when they occur. Lighting cues are LX cues and sound cues are FX. You should mark in when you give the sound and lighting operators their **standby** and **go cues**. Also mark in details of what these cues are and how long they are.

Once your group starts rehearsing the finalised work, find out when your performance date is and, by working backwards from that date, decide when your technical and dress rehearsal will be. Decide on these dates as soon as possible, to give everyone, including yourself, clear deadlines. Make sure that the space you need will be available.

It is then your job to run the technical rehearsal, working from cue to cue, and set levels and timings in consultation with the director.

The dress rehearsal should be as close to the actual performance as possible.

C *Stage manager at work on* **The Cage** *by Deborah Gearing at the Nuffield Theatre*

4

The work that you have been doing for the Controlled Assessment Task in Improvisation can count towards your final GCSE grade. If it is one of your two most successful pieces it can be put towards your Unit 2 practical work mark and if you write about it in Unit 1, the written paper, it will contribute to your final grade.

■ Unit 1: The written paper

Your work on Improvisation will be excellent for answering Section A Question 1. There are 40 marks for this answer – half of the total marks for the paper.

You need to remember that you may do this piece of work early in your course and then need to revise it for your exam. This is why all the study tips suggest that you keep notes of the work you have done so that, as well as helping with the development of the work, you will be able to use it for your written paper.

There are many ways of keeping records: a straightforward diary of progress; a series of photos; a video of your final performance; a recording of the audience's responses; and the assessment sheet of your preparation progress from your teacher.

Design and technical students will have careful notes of their progress as part of their assessment and these will be very useful.

You should be able to analyse and write about:

- the style, genre and period, the performance space and your own contribution
- what your target audience was and how they received it
- what the stimulus was and how you developed it
- the selection of what to include and how you shaped and structured the work
- the strengths and weaknesses of your own work and the whole piece.

The skills that you develop in this Controlled Assessment Task will be relevant to all other work you do which can be written about in Unit 1. For example, you will be analysing your acting skills in the same way as if you were performing a scripted role and, of course, the design and technical skills are relevant to every type of theatre. So the skills you use here will be relevant to Section B questions.

During your course, you will be given the opportunity to visit the theatre. Every time you have the opportunity to watch the work of other people in your group, you will be able to practise your audience skills. Watch carefully and note how the effects on stage have been created and why. Then when you go to the theatre you will know what to look for to answer Section C questions.

■ Unit 2: The Controlled Assessment task

The practical work is assessed by your teacher. On moderation day, an external moderator will visit your school or college to moderate your teacher's marking. Very often students do their best work when a moderator is present, so all during your course it's a good idea to have an audience for your work as well as the other people in your drama group. Maybe a teacher from another group, your head teacher or your head of year could come. This will give a sense of occasion to your performance, probably increase the pressure and result in tighter work.

Your teacher will award a mark out of 15 for the work you have done while preparing the work and a mark out of 45 for your final performance or demonstration.

During the preparation and rehearsal period, you may be involved in discussions and target-setting and you will get direction and feedback. Make sure that you take this on board. If you have sessions where other members of your group are able to watch your work and comment on it then listen carefully and respond to the help they give you. After all, the whole point of the work is to communicate your thoughts and ideas to the audience. The observers:

- may not be able to understand what is going on
- may not be able to hear
- may suggest ways of distinguishing between characters
- may have ideas about how to time an entrance or exit
- may mention health and safety issues which you have missed.

Throughout this time, you should aim to show a critical sense of your work so that you can build on the progress in each practical session.

You will be able to show a sensitive response to working in a group by listening to others, trying out their ideas and building on them, while also developing the confidence to put forward your own ideas.

You will also be able to build up a drama vocabulary as you put your work together to create a piece of theatre. Be accurate here as it will save lots of time if you all know what you are talking about.

In your final performance, you will be given credit for making sure that your performance is relevant to the style of the whole piece and your interaction on stage with the others in your group.

You will be able to show an understanding of the social context and how the development of your ideas has been communicated to the audience.

Your practical performance skills of voice, gesture and movement are credited here if you are an actor, so you will need to show your creativity and be able to sustain your performance skills through the whole piece.

If you are a designer or technician, you will show how your work is relevant to the group piece. Your contribution will be entirely relevant and your research will have been used to create appropriate work.

Your notes and designs will support the outcome and will have resulted in original and practical work.

Good luck for the performances.

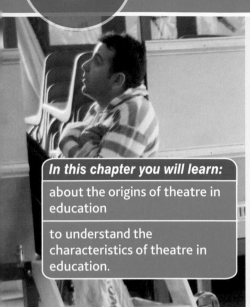
Have you ever had a visit to school from a theatre company? They probably arrived in a van with their lights, props, costumes and scenery, and performed in your school hall. Perhaps you were able to join in or had a chance to question the characters in role. If so, you have already had some experience of theatre in education.

Theatre in education (TIE) is Option 4 in the choice of Controlled Assessment options. You need to prepare for, and perform, a piece of theatre in education based on a theme designed for a specific target audience. This chapter tells you about theatre in education and helps you to devise your own theatre in education production.

In this chapter you will learn:

about the origins of theatre in education

to understand the characteristics of theatre in education.

■ Origins of theatre in education

Theatre in education was first created in Coventry, at the Belgrade Theatre, in 1965, and soon spread across Britain and the rest of the world. What made it different from other kinds of theatre was that the performers were not only actors but also trained teachers. This was important because they were employed to go into schools and use the power of theatre to make learning have a bigger impact.

■ Characteristics of theatre in education

Theatre in education is based on an educational theme. In one play, *Drink the Mercury*, the audience are led to sympathise with the family of a fisherman off the coast of Japan, who falls ill with a mysterious illness. Gradually, the audience realise that the sickness is caused by the family eating fish that had been poisoned by chemical waste containing mercury that was being pumped into the sea by a multinational company. The theme of this play is pollution.

Activities

1 Find out about the nearest theatre in education company to you. See if you can find out:

- the kinds of issues they have dealt with in the past
- the kinds of audiences they have aimed at
- the ways in which they have presented their ideas.

2 Present your findings to the rest of your group and discuss which ideas would work best for your theatre in education production.

A *An audience being entertained during a performance of* **Hamlet** *at the Orange Tree Theatre, Richmond, 2008*

After a theatre in education performance, the audience usually take part in games or workshops led by the actors. These games and workshops often involve the audience questioning the characters in role to explore why, in the story, they made particular decisions and how their decisions affected others. By becoming involved in the play, the audience develop a strong emotional reaction to the story.

Getting started

Meeting the needs of your audience

Before starting work on your theatre in education production, you will need to research the specific needs and interests of your target audience, and find the most effective ways of presenting your material to them. It will probably not be practicable to present a workshop or game after the show, but you can still keep within the original spirit of theatre in education by including in your show some way of involving your audience. See if you can build in moments of **hot-seating** or **forum theatre** that will work as part of the play.

Choosing an appropriate theme

The early theatre in education companies had teacher advisory panels made up of teachers from the schools in the area. These panels came up with ideas for shows and explained how suggested themes linked to the school curriculum. You could ask your Drama teacher to take a role as your advisory panel and to give advice on what would work in a primary school and in a secondary school.

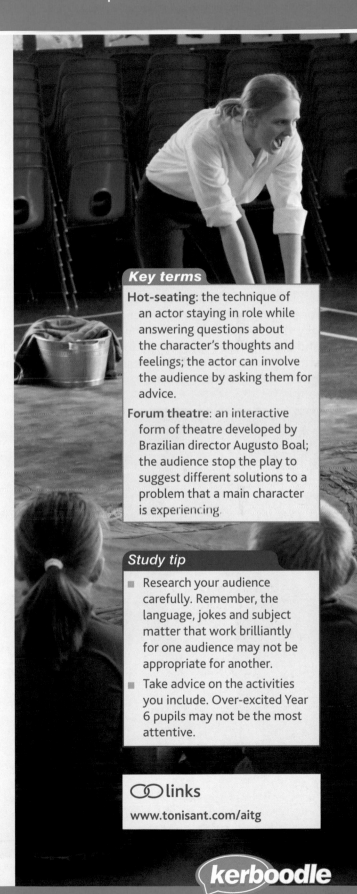

Key terms

Hot-seating: the technique of an actor staying in role while answering questions about the character's thoughts and feelings; the actor can involve the audience by asking them for advice.

Forum theatre: an interactive form of theatre developed by Brazilian director Augusto Boal; the audience stop the play to suggest different solutions to a problem that a main character is experiencing.

Study tip

- Research your audience carefully. Remember, the language, jokes and subject matter that work brilliantly for one audience may not be appropriate for another.
- Take advice on the activities you include. Over-excited Year 6 pupils may not be the most attentive.

⬤⬤ links

www.tonisant.com/aitg

kerboodle

Choose your target audience

What makes TIE different from the other options is that the production is to be prepared for a specific audience. You may choose your **target audience** yourself, perhaps the local primary schools or students from other year groups in your own school. If you feel confident, you might research a topic and perform it to your own age group or even to adults, perhaps at a parent–teacher meeting. The audience you choose will help decide the theme and style of your production.

Research your audience

Once you have decided on your target audience you will need to know the topics, issues or themes that will be most appropriate. Professional TIE companies carry out research into their target audience's needs and interests, and so must you. If, for example you have chosen to perform for primary school children attending your own school on an induction day visit, first make sure that you have permission to perform for them and find out how long your performance should last. Then find out where you can perform. Now you are committed so there is no turning back – the show *must* go on!

A *Belgrade Theatre, Coventry – working closely with the target audience*

Key terms

Target audience: the specific audience (defined, for example, by age or interest) for which a production is devised.

Activities

1 Remember how you felt on your first day at school and present it as a monologue.

2 a Work on improvised scenes between a pupil and a parent.

   b Plan how you might use these in a TIE production.

Study tip

- Find out the needs of your target audience.
- Write them down on posters placed in your Drama room.
- Keep referring to them to keep 'on track'.
- Consult frequently with your Drama teacher.

Research your theme

Changing schools always raises hopes and fears. Ask the head of Year 7 what problems are frequently faced by new pupils and what your school does to help solve them. See if you can contact their primary school teachers for advice, and make sure you have planned your questions carefully – these are busy people. Some of your group may have younger brothers and sisters who can help in your research and all of you were once new pupils. You can draw upon and share your own experiences. Starting school is an important part of growing up and you will be able to find much material in biographies, novels and plays.

Research your materials

During your research, you may find material that is relevant, and this could help you decide on the direction you take in devising your production. A good start is the play *Daisy Pulls it Off*, by Denise Deegan.

In the first act, the heroine arrives at her new boarding school and encounters the school bullies. The period is the 1920s and the style is deliberately exaggerated, with period slang and direct addresses to the audience. This style contrasts with that of the novel and play *Kes!*, by Barry Hines. Set in a Yorkshire secondary school in the 1960s, it is more naturalistic in style and language. Both offer set pieces such as confrontations with authority, bullies and the games field, which could be set against each other for contrast. Amongst these you would be able to knit together material drawn from your own experiences and shaped to fit your production. Though the style is not realistic, audiences can recognise the emotions as being true to life.

So far we have looked at the topic of starting a new school from the point of view of the pupils. Remember that in every situation there are other viewpoints. Think about how the parents might feel, or imagine what it might be like to be a head of Year 7 faced with coping with a new intake. Whatever theme or topic you choose, you will need to consider and include a range of different viewpoints in order to show **balance** in your production.

Activity

3 a Collect a range of written materials on your chosen theme. First day at school would do as an example.

 b Choose short extracts and organise them into a possible running order.

 c Improvise links between the extracts.

 d Improvise your own version of extracts that are not easy to present in performance.

Remember

It might be helpful to look back at Chapter 2 and Chapter 4 to remind you of the practical skills you can use. Upstart Theatre use devising as a technique. Look at *Focus Group* on their website for blogs and photographs of how a show develops.

Key terms

Balance: giving fair attention to other viewpoints so that the production is seen to be unbiased; this is very important when dealing with controversial topics.

B   **Daisy Pulls it Off**, *performed at the Lyric Theatre, London in 2002*

Work as a group

The first TIE companies worked co-operatively, with everyone contributing to the devising and writing of the production. This approach works well for GCSE Drama students and means that everyone can have a say in the way the piece is formed. It is always important for the design and technical contributors to be closely involved in the planning. In TIE, contributions such as offering ideas for costume, set or lighting can help shape the way the show develops. There are scripts available which are suitable for TIE, such as *Too Much Punch for Judy* and others in that series.

Involve your audience

It has already been stated that what makes TIE different from other options is audience involvement. Involvement can take many forms, and it is a good idea to try and find as many ways as possible and then choose the most appropriate. Here are a few ideas to start you off – develop them to fit your skills and the needs of your audience and your show.

Give your audience a role

One of the simplest approaches is to start by giving your audience a role in the production. You might wish to explain to them before the show that they will be treated as a jury, for example, and will have to vote on a decision at the end of the show. More subtly, they can be greeted at the start of the show by an actor **in role** who welcomes them, for example, as members of the council planning committee and explains that they will have to make a decision based on what they are about to see. The approach you choose will depend on your confidence in yourselves as performers and your confidence in the audience's ability to accept you.

Involve your audience's sympathy

If you choose the starting school topic from the previous page, you might wish to present your show through a character that the audience might sympathise with. Perhaps the production could be centred on someone who is frightened at the thought of going into secondary school and who shows all the anxieties that were revealed from your audience research. If the character seems more anxious than members of the audience, it is likely that they will be sympathetic. The character could address them and ask for advice at key moments and help them feel involved.

In rehearsals, members of the group who are not performers could usefully take on the role of audience and ask questions or give advice. This can help keep designers or technical crew involved with the process of shaping the piece and will give them a wider range of material to draw upon when they come to face the written examination. It also helps the performers as they can be prepared for different kinds of response from their audience.

Objectives

In this section you will learn to:

recognise the need to plan as a group

find ways of involving the audience constructively.

Remember

- Don't be over-ambitious. Only try approaches that you and your group are comfortable with.
- Consult with your Drama teacher and those who know your audience well. Take notice of their advice.

Key terms

In role: appearing convincingly and consistently as a character different from oneself.

Study tip

Remember to keep notes of your planning process:

- what you did
- how you did it
- why you did it.

You need this to answer questions in Section A of Unit 1, the written paper.

Experiment with hot-seating

Hot-seating, or having an actor in role answering questions from the audience, can be a very effective way of involving your audience. You may already be experienced in the technique from your work in improvisation, in which case it should not be too difficult to apply it in live performance. If not, use it as a tool in rehearsals to help you create a rounded **characterisation**. Don't consider using the technique until you feel absolutely confident that you can respond comfortably as your character in all situations.

A *The Belgrave Theatre, Coventry – a tense moment. Hot-seating can be a helpful preparation*

Hot-seating can be used effectively at the end of a performance by giving an audience a chance to ask characters about their **motivation**. During the show, hot-seating can help an audience to understand why something is happening. Experiment when you are in the safety of rehearsals and see what ideas come out. Follow leads and be flexible; do not plan everything on paper first. TIE is practical – do it!

Activity

1 a Choose a character you have played in a scripted play or improvisation.

   b Think of ten questions you would like to ask the character that were not answered in the piece you performed.

   c Write down what you think your character would have replied to each question.

   d Try answering questions from members of your group. Start simply until you become confident.

Remember

Look at pages 42–45 for further help on creating characters. Look at scripts such as *No Punch for Judy* or *Drink the Mercury* for ideas.

Study tip

If you decide to perform a published TIE script, your option will become Acting, not theatre in education.

Preparing for the show

◼ Organising your theatre in education show

In TIE, careful organisation and planning is essential. You will have to research your audience and materials to fit and support your chosen theme or topic and will have to consider ways in which to involve your audience. However, involving the audience directly can throw up unexpected problems, so it is safest to be prepared. In TIE the actors also function as teachers and carry the same responsibilities that teachers have when preparing lessons and controlling classes. When in doubt ask your teacher for help and advice.

◼ Plan your audience management

First, you will need to consider how your audience might behave. If they are familiar with TIE there is unlikely to be a problem. If they are not, then you will need to consider how best to manage your audience. Even the most inexperienced performer can 'wind up' an audience to the point where they are all calling out and not listening. It takes skill to get them quiet and attentive again. Throwing sweets into the audience may be fun at a pantomime, but may be less so if you are wanting the audience to listen to an important point you have to make in a TIE show, never mind the health and safety implications …

Objectives

In this section you will learn to:

organise a theatre in education production

plan audience management

consider performance spaces.

A *An actress involving her audience during the Orange Tree performance of* **Hamlet**

You will need to plan how you will manage the audience when it arrives. In a theatre the audience arrives and you perform. In TIE there are many more possibilities open to you.

It may be possible to arrange the audience into smaller groups, each led into the performance space by an actor who can talk to them informally while still in role. The actor can then act as leader and focus for the group, feeding them ideas and offering particular viewpoints. Smaller numbers mean that the group can feel more confident about contributing ideas. Also, each group can have slightly different viewpoints, which will make it easier for having discussions at the end, if that is how you wish to end your show.

■ Choose your performance space to fit the show

Think about the performance space you use. This could be led by the needs of the show, for example, in a playground if your audience research into 'starting school' suggested that most of the audience was anxious about being bullied there on their first day. The audience could be led by sympathetic characters into the playground where the rest of the cast are already performing as bullies. The action could be frozen by a character playing the teacher blowing a whistle or ringing a bell. It is always a good idea to make sure that the roles of characters that have to lead the audience or give instructions have a high **status** so that what they say will be listened to and acted upon. Actors could then move onto the performance space and perform their parts until the next whistle.

Activity

1
a   Make a list of the tasks your group will need to do in preparation for your theatre in education Controlled Assessment.

b   Number the tasks in order of when they will need to be done.

c   Against each activity write the names of the members of your group who you think will best complete that task. Don't use the same name twice!

d   Plan how you will complete your task.

e   Draw up a tick list to help you check when you have completed your tasks.

Study tip

In your planning, make sure that you share out the parts fairly and that everyone has sufficient exposure on stage.

Key terms

Status: the relative position or standing of someone in a group to others; for example, a ship's captain has a higher status than the surgeon but a lower status when the captain is ill.

◯◯ links

www.pwynne.hostinguk.com/TIE.htm

B   *Students going through a final check before the performance*

Devising your show

Turn your research into a production

So far we have looked at the things that make theatre in education productions different from those in the other performance options. Now we will look at putting material together into a show – what the companies call **devising**. If you have worked on Option 1 Devised thematic work, you will already know how extracts from playscripts, poems or prose can be fitted together with original work that you and your group have produced. In theatre in education, you can just use original work that you and your group have improvised or written if you wish.

Theatre in education is about commitment to your audience and the theme that will be appropriate for them. Your group will need to agree firmly on the theme. Ask yourselves the questions:

- Why have you chosen the topic?
- Why is it important, both to your audience and you?

If you can answer these questions confidently, then you are ready to devise.

Have a group meeting where everyone involved shares their research and ideas. Write these down on large sheets of paper and pin them up on the wall. Spider diagrams, sketches, photocopies of play extracts, and photographs can all be pinned up with notes in different coloured marker pens to help keep track of ideas and also show the contributions that sound, lighting and design candidates wish to make.

- Always keep your target audience in mind.
- Think about **audience participation** so that you can involve them directly in the show.
- Remember that you have a responsibility to your audience – if they are apprehensive about starting a new school, then you will need to focus on ways to reassure them.

Experiment through improvisation

Earlier, we chose 'starting school' as an example because it is a topic that is very familiar. The way in which we looked at that idea is the same for any topic. Out of the research will come ideas. These can be developed through further research as you add to or replace written materials. *Tom Brown's Schooldays*, by Thomas Arnold, *Nicholas Nickleby*, by Charles Dickens, or Roald Dahl's *Boy* might give material on bullying or unsympathetic headmasters that could be quoted, acted out or used as a starting point for improvisations.

The ideas raised from talking to people or remembering your own experiences of starting school, for example, will give you very useful starting points for improvisations. The Activity box will give you some starter ideas.

Objectives

In this section you will learn to:

turn research materials into a production

make a commitment to audience and material

work as a group

experiment through improvisation

shape the material.

Skills study

Look at Peter Wynne-Wilson's 'Notes on the Divising Process' at www.pwynne.hostinguk.com/TIE.htm.

Key terms

Devising: planning a production and working out how it can be performed effectively.

Audience participation: directly involving the audience in the production, for example, by asking them questions or giving individuals simple tasks.

Activity

1 Improvise scenes involving a new pupil and a parent:

a   In a shoe shop buying uniform shoes – the new pupil insists on something fashionable, the parent doesn't want to buy them.

b   5.00 am on the first day – the pupil is in uniform, the parent is in bed …

c   Breakfast time, next day. The pupil starts with 'I don't feel well enough to go to school …'

Shape your material

Once you have collected the materials, you will need to give them a structure so that they make sense to the audience and fit together in a satisfying way. Basically, it needs a beginning, middle and end. In the case of 'starting school' you will want your audience to leave happy, reassured and wanting to come back in September, so the end might be the section you think about first. Perhaps you would devise a cheerful, upbeat song and dance number in which members of the cast take groups away to meet friendly pupils and discuss what they have seen. The worst approach is to start at the beginning and rehearse the opening over and over until you realise it's two days from the show and you still have not done the ending.

Consider beginnings and ends

Carefully plan your opening scene and grab the audience's interest and attention. Whether you have a shock or comic start make sure that the next scene is different in tone and mood. Earlier we looked at audience management. Remember that the structure of your production can help by following exciting actions with quiet, calming moments.

Study tip

It is better to improvise work as a group because:

■ You will be able to demonstrate your skills development for your Part 1 practical assessment.

■ You will have more material to answer Question 1 in Unit 1, the written paper.

Remember

Look at Chapter 2 for useful approaches. Look at the website of Upstart Theatre to see how a professional company works at devising a show.

∞links

http://spa.exeles.ac.uk/drama/links/theatreedu.htm

A *Belgrade Theatre Coventry* – **The First Time I Saw Snow**

As a performer in this option you will have to prepare for, and perform, a piece of theatre in education based on a theme designed for a specific target audience. The audience could be of any age, but you must recognise and cater for the specific needs of your audience and choose approaches that will make the impact of your work most effective. These are aspects that have been covered in this chapter so far.

■ What you have to do

The specification says that the work can include the target audience and lead to further exploration of the theme or topic with the intended audience. Professional companies usually include a workshop to follow their productions. While it is good professional practice to do this, you need to remember that these are companies with trained actor-teachers. Whatever follow-up you decide upon it is worth bearing in mind that the examination cannot take into account your teaching skills, as:

- you are not a trained teacher
- the marking criteria cover performance aspects, rather than teaching skills.

Your focus needs to be completely on your performance to your audience, what you do and how you do it. However successfully you organise a workshop session with games or a discussion, you will not gain more marks if your actual performing skills do not fit in with the marking criteria.

■ The skills you will need

The performance skills examined are no different from those used in the other performance options and one particular advantage of choosing theatre in education is that it offers you a chance to draw upon all the skills you have learnt. Devising skills learnt in Option 1 Devised thematic work can be linked with acting, improvisation and physical theatre skills.

■ Experiment with styles

It is worth mentioning style again at this point. Each production will require a different approach, and even as you work on a particular show you can usefully experiment with style. Once you have a clear idea of the shape of the piece and the material you are going to use you can start to rehearse using different approaches.

Documentary

Documentary style involves presenting the material in a balanced, factual way, as if in a serious television programme. This is particularly appropriate for topics based on real-life incidents, perhaps featuring

A *Belgrade Theatre, Coventry – engaging the audience with live music in* **The First Time I Saw Snow**

real people. Dramatised flashbacks might be presented in a serious, naturalistic style, for example, in *A Memory of Lizzie* in *Sepia and Song*, by David Foxton.

Pantomime

You could be able to present your material in the style of a pantomime, using stock characters such as the Fairy Godmother (or play with the names to produce the Hairy Godfather for instance, as a mafia-type villain). Here, instead of naturalism, the characters would be presented as caricatures with broad gestures. They might follow the traditional pantomime conventions of a principal boy played by a female and the dame played by a male.

Melodrama

Melodrama is a variation on pantomime based on a 19th-century theatre style that evolved when theatres could only perform plays if they had a Royal Warrant. Unlicensed theatres got around the law by performing their plays with musical backing. These plays often had clearly defined heroines and villains, each with their own theme music and using an over-dramatic acting style with spoken asides to the audience. A good example for you to look at is *Maria Marten or Murder in the Red Barn*, based on a real event in Victorian times.

> **Remember**
>
> Whatever style you finally decide upon, make sure it is appropriate to your piece and your audience. Above all be consistent and enjoy the closer relationship you will have with your audience.

> **Study tip**
>
> Always offer your strongest performance skills for examination.
> Keep a record of what you do and record details of how and why.

5.6 Option 6: Set design

You can offer your set design skills as part of a TIE project. You will have to prepare and present a scale model of a set suitable for the TIE project produced by the group you are working in. It may be that practical considerations make it impossible for you to produce a full usable set for the actual show, although, if you can, it would be helpful to the performers. If not, in addition to your model, you will be expected to prepare the performance space as close as possible to your designs and dress it appropriately.

Be practical

Your designs will have to be practical. Show that you have thought about the needs of the production. This means that you will need to think about how you would build the set, if you had the time and materials to do so. The set will have to be used by actors in performance so it needs to be able to help them, giving them clear entrances and exits as well as space in which to move.

Keep to the theme

You will also need to think about the theme of the production and how the set can help convey this to an audience. You could use distinct images that the audience will immediately recognise, for example, the Eiffel Tower and Paris.

Work as part of the team

As a designer you will work as part of the group. Many TIE companies work as 'integrated companies', in which each person, though a specialist in a particular area, such as design, will also carry out other tasks. Be prepared to be involved in rehearsals as an audience member, helping with hot-seating or as an extra character as the actors explore their characters and ideas. You will also need to play an active part in the devising process, for example, by taking part in improvisations. You will be able to suggest solutions to staging and presentation problems and also feel more involved in the show. The more experience you have of preparation and planning the material, the better scope you will have for attempting Question 1 in the written paper.

Fit in with other design elements

Your designs for the set will have to fit in with the lighting, costumes, puppets, masks and properties. As a group you will have discussed style and made decisions. From that point all the design team will need to work together to make sure that style, materials and colours fit together and do not clash with each other. The production may be set in a particular period or show different moods or atmospheres and you will have to research ways of showing these through your designs.

Study tip

Be aware of:

- health and safety issues
- the needs of the actors
- the needs of the audience
- period, mood, atmosphere, style.

■ Consider the challenges of touring

TIE gives designers particular challenges because it often involves touring from venue to venue. Many schools devise TIE shows that they tour to a number of their feeder primary schools. This means that the set will have to be portable and capable of being fitted into a school minibus or a transit van.

One solution could be to use folding screens fitted together with pin hinges. Collapsible **rostra** can be used to give differences in heights.

■ Check your venues first

If your group is to tour then visit every venue and take measurements not only of performance areas but also doors and wing space. Check seating areas for sight lines. If you are using projection check that there are suitable screens, available power points and that your equipment is compatible with that of the venue.

After you have made your first sketches draw your final designs. Draw up a **ground plan** to scale and use this plan as a basis for your scale model of the set.

> **Remember**
>
> If you are using a vehicle to transport your set, measure its doors and internal space before building your set!

> **Key terms**
>
> **Rostrum (plural rostra):** a portable platform which you can use to create interesting levels.
>
> **Ground plan:** a scale outline of the set drawn as if from above with indications of flats and furniture marked on it.

A *University of Derby,* **The Shadow Box**. *A simple way of showing different locations and suitable for touring*

5.7 Option 7: Costume design

Costume design can fit very well into a theatre in education project. For the practical part of the examination you will have to prepare, and complete or **assemble**, a costume that is entirely your own work. You will also have to provide designs for at least one other costume for the same production.

Plan closely with your group

You will need to work closely with the others in your group from the start of the project. Offer suggestions and also listen to others. Your job is to help communicate the ideas and style of the show as well as the period in which it is set and the status and mood of the characters. Make notes and sketches as you go, and keep them for reference and for revision for the written paper. They will also be helpful for your teacher when your Part 1 mark is given.

Find out what clothes say about people

The clothes people wear tell us something about them – their age, social class, job, wealth, interests and even nationality. You can see this for yourself if you watch people in your school and note what they wear and how they wear it. See how many variations of school uniform are visible in one class, for example, and think about what each variation tells you about the wearer. As a designer, you will have to interpret the characters in your production and find ways of showing an audience who they are and what they are like.

Research the character and consider materials

The group discussions about style will give you a start, and you will need to discuss with the actors how the character will be played. Plan a colour scheme and think about fabrics and textures that will support your final ideas. As a designer you can help influence the acting performance – for example, by giving the heroine a pale and lightweight fabric that floats on the air as she moves to contrast with the dark, rough textures of the villain. If you can, improvise or read the

A *Costume design for* **Looking for JJ**, *Pilot Theatre, York*

part in rehearsals to see what it feels like to play the character. Discuss your ideas with the set designer to make sure that colours and styles work with each other. Consult with the lighting designer and check the effect the lights have on your chosen fabrics – a smart red cloak will look black under green lighting.

Research the period

If your production is set in a particular period, then you will need to research the clothes worn. Look at books on the history of costume, art books, photographs, paintings, postcards as well as on the internet. Keep details of your research. Consider the style of your production. Is it naturalistic? If so, you may wish to have your costumes as historically accurate as you can manage. Otherwise, you may be able to indicate period through details of **accessories** such as hats, or through the overall shape of the costume. The main things to consider are whether it effectively communicates what you want it to and whether it also looks right.

Experiment through sketches

Experiment with ideas by drawing sketches: it is the designer's particular form of improvisation. Keep them and work them into finished designs adding swatches of fabric to give others a clear image of what you intend.

Make or assemble

As you will need to make or assemble one of your designs, you must consider the practicalities. You will need to:

- take the measurements of the actor
- obtain the appropriate fabrics
- find suitable patterns
- sew and fit the garment,

If you are not sewing the costume, you will need to:

- source the individual parts of the costume
- assemble them on the actor.

Study tip

Keep your working notes together and in date order so that you can demonstrate to your teacher how you worked in the planning and preparation stages and why you made your decisions.
Work out costs and keep records.

Key terms

Accessories: items of clothing such as hats, belts, ties or jewellery that add to the overall effect of a costume.

Did you know ???????

In early black-and-white Western movies, the audience knew who the bad guys were as they wore black hats while the 'goodies' wore pale colours. This is an example of a design convention.

B **Looking for JJ** – *What do the costumes tell you about the characters?*

5.8 Option 8: Make-up

Make-up can be offered for all five performance options. In theatre in education you will have to prepare and present **two** contrasting make-ups which are your own work. Because of the need to produce contrasting designs you will have to make sure that the production offers you scope to do this effectively. You are free to make up yourself or another person.

■ Research different materials and products

You will need to find out about the different kinds of stage make-up that are in use, even if you are very familiar with one particular kind. One health and safety factor is the fact that some people are allergic to certain products such as greasepaint, so it is important to be able to offer alternatives. If you are new to this skill you must also find out about basic make-up hygiene.

A *Kate from Rhubarb Theatre's* **Cooking with Kate** *made-up as an older person*

Experiment with styles

As part of your background research, experiment with different styles of make-up, such as character or fantasy, particularly as these offer opportunities to create the necessary contrast. Knowledge of specialist make-up, such as wounds and injuries, might even be useful: for example, the ghost of Banquo in *Macbeth*. The St John Ambulance Brigade have an injury simulation kit and can provide training.

Work as part of the group

During the group planning meetings and rehearsals, this knowledge should enable you to contribute ideas for presentation, and you will need to keep a record with notes, sketches and photographs of how these change and develop. All theatre involves **illusion**, and make-up can play a vital part in creating and sustaining this. A particular problem in school productions of any sort is the fact that the actors often have to play characters much older than themselves. Effective make-up can make actors seem more convincing and can help them get more quickly into character. Changes to an actor's appearance might have to be extreme, using **prosthetics** to change the shape of a nose, for example. Even if your production does not require this, it will be a useful part of your research notes if you can demonstrate your knowledge and understanding.

∞ links

www.stjohnssupplier.co.uk and click on training aids.

Key terms

Illusion: anything that deceives the senses by appearing to be something which it is not.

Prosthetics: artificial body parts; an example in stage make-up could be nose-putty, moulded to change the shape of a nose then coloured by make-up.

B *Make-up: Tigger from HumDrum's production of* **Winnie the Pooh**

Study tip

Make sure that your make-up fits the style of the production.

5.9 Option 9: Properties

Stage properties (props) are any objects, apart from the set, that are used in a production. For this option you will need to prepare and present **two** different stage properties for use in the theatre in education show. The props will have to be used in the actual show and be made entirely by you.

These are the activities you will need to be able to carry out when you start work on a TIE production:

■ Take a play text and make a note of every prop that is mentioned in the text. In a TIE piece you would make notes in a rehearsal and ask the group what period, style, shape or size it should be and how it is to be used.

■ List all props carefully on a sheet of paper with page or line references next to them.

■ Write 'Personal' and the character's name against those that are used solely by one character. The actor will have to be responsible for looking after these and may even be able to find them for you.

■ Write down possible sources of the props you think you will be able to find.

■ Write 'Make' against those you will have to make.

Think how you might construct each of them as you will have to prepare two different props for your Controlled Assessment.

Research widely

You will need to show that you know how and why props are used in the theatre and know how to obtain and make them. As productions can cover a range of historical periods you will need to know about period style so that your items fit in and are convincing.

You must be practical and organised and take an active part in the planning. Take notes and make suggestions; research the chosen topic and the period in which your production is set. At rehearsals, keep notes on every object that is mentioned and list who uses them and when. This will be the basis of your props list.

Personal props

Personal props are used by a particular actor and are set out in the dressing room before a performance. Some of these will be provided by the actor, others you will have to find. Get into the habit of making them available from the start of rehearsals and of collecting them in and recording them on your props list.

Study tip

Always make sure that your props fit the style and needs of the production.

Props can be borrowed or hired. Friends, family or local businesses can sometimes be willing to help for a mention in your programme. Take a receipt book and record full details of the lender, the value and condition and give a receipt. State when you'll return them and do so promptly.

Making props

Some properties you will have to make yourself: these are called **makes**. Learn methods of construction such as using chicken wire and papier-mâché or expanded polystyrene. Your CDT, resistant materials and art departments should be able to offer you help and advice. Before you start make sure you have technical support such as materials, tools, work space and advice, as well as advice on health and safety.

Key terms

Makes: items that cannot be found or borrowed and must therefore be made.

A   *A variety of props*

Finding props

The prop you construct has to look realistic on stage. It will be used in rehearsals and must be sturdy enough to last through the rehearsals and for the run of the show without falling apart or looking tatty.

Activity

1 a   List the props that you have decided on so far, with a note of where they come from, who uses them in the production and which scenes they are used in.

   b   Sketch the items you will make and draw up a list of materials you need.

   c   Get feedback from the performers on your ideas.

5.10 Option 10: Masks and Option 11: Puppets

Masks and puppets can be used very effectively in TIE and the skills needed for design and construction are very similar. Both could be used powerfully in the same production.

Objectives

In this section you will learn to:

research the chosen option fully

co-operate closely with others in the group

experiment with styles and materials.

▉ Course requirements for Option 10

You will have to prepare and present **two** contrasting masks to be used in the TIE performance. You have to work as part of the group and the masks must be your own work. Note that the masks must be contrasting.

▉ Course requirements for Option 11

You will have to prepare and present a puppet for a theatre in education performance.

You will need to keep notes on your research, discussions with the group and the progress of your designs from sketches to completion. These will show your knowledge and understanding for your Part 1 mark and will help you work out your final designs.

▉ Research your skills option

Before you start work on the production, research the history of theatre masks or puppets and find out about companies that use them today. Look at the range of styles you can use and consider their strengths and weaknesses from the point of view of your own TIE project. Find out methods of construction and materials you need.

A *Masks used to give the illusion of insects*

Work as part of the group

Working with others in the group is essential. From your research you can contribute ideas and suggest solutions to problems of presentation, but be realistic. Wearing masks or working puppets in performance needs special skills, so from an early stage work closely with the actors. You may need to provide temporary stand-in masks for rehearsals while you work on your finished products. Adapt your designs and ideas to fit the skills of the performers. Consult often with the set, costume, props and lighting designers to make sure your designs will fit together.

Study tip

Make sure that your masks or puppets are practical and can be used safely and expressively by the performer.

Think about the characters or moods they need to show and find ways of including these in your design.

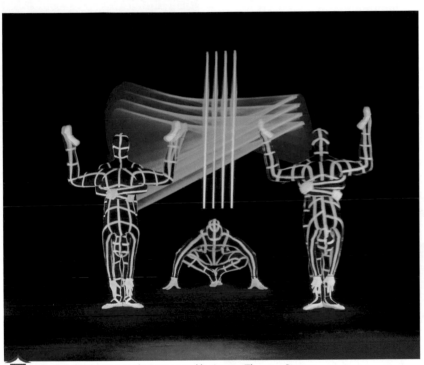

B   *Black light theatre techniques used by Image Theatre, Prague*

Think about style

Masks and puppets can be very effective in productions that have a fantasy style or involve elements such as dreams or magic. Impressive effects can be created quite simply and inexpensively. With the help of your lighting designer it may be possible to experiment with **black light** theatre to create effective underwater or space sequences using ultraviolet (UV) lamps and special paint against a plain black background. The darkness can hide puppeteers from view and variations of size can be suggested by having puppets alongside masked actors wearing **luminescent** costumes. If you are touring several venues and using UV effects, check that the performance space can be blacked out completely.

Key terms

Black light: use of ultraviolet lamps that cause specially treated surfaces to glow vividly when switched on; it is effective in puppetry and to give the effect of objects flying or moving by themselves on stage.

Luminescent: a word that describes an item that glows in the dark when ultraviolet light is switched on.

5.11 Option 12: Lighting and Option 13: Sound

Lighting and sound are technical design options. They are grouped together here because they offer similar challenges and the preparation processes are similar. You will need to have use of a range of technical equipment and have the use of a technician to rig, under your direction, any equipment that is beyond normal reach.

Course requirements for Option 12

You will have to prepare and present the lighting for an actual TIE project. For Part 1 you should keep all your notes, including your lighting plots, rigging diagrams, scripts or running order, as well as risk assessment sheets, to show that you understand the job and are aware of health and safety matters.

Examiners will be looking to see that you understand how and when different types of lanterns such as **focus spots**, **fresnels** or **parcans** are used and that you are familiar with the use of the lighting board, dimmer packs and **patching**. You will need to know how to create effects by using **colour filters**, **effects projectors** and **gobos** and how these can change the appearance of costumes and set. Finally, you will have to choose the lighting that is most appropriate for the show and that helps convey its mood and atmosphere.

A *Checking the lighting*

Objectives

In this section you will learn to:

research the chosen option fully

co-operate closely with others in the group

experiment with styles and materials.

Key terms

Focus spot: light on a specific area of the stage, for example on a specific character.

Fresnel: (pronounced fre-nel) the most common type of lantern used on stage, it has a textured lens and produces a very even light that is soft at the edges and tends to project a soft shadow.

Parcan: a lantern that is used to provide strong dramatic keylight, backlight or effects such as beams of light in smoke.

Patching: connecting stage lights (lanterns) to dimmer controls for fading in and out.

Colour filter: a coloured film placed in front of a lantern to change the colour of the light on stage (also known as a gel).

Effects projector: a device used to project an image from a rotating glass disc to give the effect of, for example, clouds, flames or rain.

Gobo: a small metal plate inserted behind a spotlight to project an image onto the stage.

⊂⊃**links**

www.partnersinrhyme.com/pir/
PIRsfx.shtml

Course requirements for Option 13

You will have to prepare and present a **sound plot** for an actual TIE project. For Part 1 you should keep all your notes, sound plots, choice of effects or music, scripts or running order, as well as risk assessment sheets, to show that you understand the job and are aware of health and safety matters.

Examiners will be looking to see that you understand the importance of sound effects and music in a production and the ways in which different moods and atmospheres can be created. You will therefore need to be able to choose, even create, the sounds required and know how to record, mix and edit them and control their levels in performance.

Research your skills option

However much previous experience you may have had, start by researching your option to find out how others work, and check catalogues to see what equipment is currently available for sale or hire. Even if you can't afford it, make notes to show that you know about it and know how it might have been used. A useful starting point is the Partners in Rhyme, which offers a large range of effects for free.

Work as part of the group and experiment with style

Work as a team player in your group and offer ideas of how your skills can help the production work more effectively. Research the topic from the point of view of lighting or sound and find ways of supporting the style and moods of the piece. Carefully chosen lighting effects using gobos and subtle recordings of birdsong can create a dappled and friendly wood. By lowering intensities and **cross-fading** to dark blues the mood can change to a sense of menace as birdsong fades to eerie music. Loud, cheerful music and bright colours on a **colour wheel** will change the mood yet again and give a carnival style. Experiment with colours, live and recorded sounds, levels and rates of fading and share the results with your group.

Think about problems of touring

If the performance is held in your own school you will have familiar equipment at hand. On tour things can be more of a problem. Check the venues physically and enquire about the equipment available and whether you are allowed to use it. If you are, make arrangements to practise before the tour. Make sure that the equipment is compatible with your requirements. Check all power points and calculate the **safe load** available for lighting, sound equipment and other electrical appliances that you wish to use. Do not risk overloading the system.

> **Key terms**
>
> **Sound plot**: a list of sound cues and levels in running order.
>
> **Colour wheel**: a disc of coloured filters that rotates to produce a rainbow effect.
>
> **Cross-fading**: when one lighting state goes out at exactly the same time as another one comes on.
>
> **Safe load**: the maximum weight that should be put onto a lifting device or suspension point.

> **Study tip**
>
> Always follow health and safety rules.
> Tape down loose cables.
> Keep notes of what you have done.

5.12 Option 14: Stage management

In TIE, you will have all the responsibilities of preparing for and running the show and organising its tour. You will need to be level-headed, efficient, organised, inventive and tactful with people. As you may have to supervise some rehearsals you will need to be creative and be able to interpret clearly the director's or group's artistic intentions. You have to keep everything together and working, solving and avoiding problems, making sure that everything happens just at the right time, then clearing up afterwards. It's a tall order, but for the right person it can be the most satisfying role in the production.

For this option, as a stage manager you will have to prepare for and 'run the show' for an actual theatre in education presentation. You will need to produce a range of documents and notes including the prompt copy or stage manager's book (details of this are on page 85 in Chapter 4, Improvisation). These will be needed not only to help you do your job efficiently but also to demonstrate your knowledge and understanding of stage management.

Objectives

In this section you will learn to:

research the chosen option fully

co-operate closely with the rest of the group

co-ordinate everyone's efforts.

■ Document everything

As stage manager you will need to be at the core of the group taking notes on artistic and technical decisions and researching the background to the show. These can be kept in your production file. It will be handy to have copies of properties lists, **ground plan**, wardrobe lists, lighting and sound cues and contact details of cast and crew in case someone is late. Documents you will need to produce include:

- production schedule, starting with first meeting and ending with clearing-up post production; on it you need to include deadlines for each of the design and technical departments and details of all performance times and dates;
- **rehearsal schedule** of all rehearsals including technical, costume call and dress rehearsals;
- ground plan drawn to scale if not produced by the set designer;
- prompt copy with cues for lighting (LX), special effects (FX) and sound effects (SX), entered in the correct order with details of moves;
- production risk assessment with details of potential hazards, risk involved and means of avoiding them;
- to do list – the most important tool for each week – split into days and jobs with the most urgent, difficult or time-consuming placed at the top;
- stage manager's report after each performance noting problems and solutions.

Key terms

Ground plan: a scale outline of the set drawn as if from above with indications of flats and furniture marked on it.

Rehearsal schedule: a list of times and places of rehearsals with the names of actors who are needed.

Get in: moving everything from storage and van onto the stage and preparing for the performance.

Get out: removing everything from the stage to storage or van.

Know about everything

You will have to be able to name all backstage equipment and know what it does, why it is being used in this production and who is responsible for it. This will include both design elements such as set, costume and properties, and technical equipment such as lanterns, smoke machines and microphones. Frequent contact with the team will help you to do this, as well as personal research.

A   *The stage manager at work*

Organise everything

If you are taking your show on tour, draw up a touring schedule. Record contact details of venues and details of transport in your production file as well as copies of maps, and plans of performance areas. Risk assessment and parent consent forms will need to be completed.

Check and measure each venue and plan transport for cast, crew, set, lighting, sound, costumes and props. Organise their packing. If the venue is within walking distance, plan who carries what. If you need transport arrange this well in advance with a responsible member of staff. If possible, be first at the venue to set up, giving your group plenty of time to get ready. Delegate jobs and make sure everyone knows what to do, and does it. It is helpful to practise setting and striking before leaving for the **get in**.

Manage the **get out** making sure that everyone helps clear up, with each department, such as costume, lighting or set, taking responsibility for its own area.

5

Every Controlled Assessment Task you complete can count towards your final grade, even if it is not selected as one of your best two practical marks, because you can write about it in Unit 1, the written paper. This means that every practical project can be a preparation for Unit 1 and should be taken seriously.

■ Unit 1: The written paper

Unit 1 has three sections. You must complete Section A, Question 1, which is compulsory. You can then choose from Section B, study and performance of a scripted play, and Section C, study of a live production seen.

Theatre in education is not based on a scripted play and so it can only be offered as answer material for Section A, Question 1. This asks you to write about any practical work you have done as part of the course. You will already have collected much preparation material for your project for the Unit 2 Part 1 assessment which will be marked by your teacher. When you are revising for Unit 1 you can organise this material to fit the kinds of questions that will be set.

Question 1 is in four parts, each of which is worth 10 marks. Make each point clearly and briefly.

1a) asks you to describe what you did in your practical piece and examiners will expect you to mention some of the following:

- Style – did you use documentary, fantasy, realism or perhaps a mixture of these?
- Genre – in your case it will be theatre in education. Mention briefly what makes TIE different.
- Period in which your TIE show was set. Was it set in the past, present or future?
- Target audience. Here you will be able to state whether you chose peers, adults or primary school children.
- Performance space. This might have involved several kinds of space from end-on stage to in the round. Keep it brief, with clear details.
- Your own contribution: for example, actor, designer of set, costumes, props, lighting, sound, or stage manager. Again, give a clear and brief comment.

1b) asks you to explain what you did. Examiners will look for:

- your first ideas, such as how you chose your theme and style and how this led to thinking about performance spaces and equipment
- practical details of the ways in which you worked
- how you and your group researched your audience and its needs
- practical details of the techniques you used, improvising and experimenting with materials and ideas

■ explanation of how you used these techniques to develop and show off your skills.

1c) asks for an explanation of the ways in which you worked and why things were done in that way.

1d) asks you to evaluate the success of your work and/or that of others. Think about this question as you do your practical work and note down your opinions along with your reasons.

■ Unit 2: The Controlled Assessment task

Your practical work will be assessed by your teacher whose marking will be checked by a visiting moderator who will come to your centre and mark a sample of candidates. The assessment is in two parts.

Part 1

Before the moderation day your teacher will mark your preparation work out of 15 based on how you were seen to have worked and on the quality of your planning notes mentioned earlier in this chapter. The specification calls this 'process and understanding of skills development'.

To gain high marks, make sure that you always:

■ contribute positively

■ make detailed notes and sketches and keep all documents and records

■ show evidence of research and experiment

■ show awareness of health and safety

■ show awareness of how your skill links with others

■ show commitment to the project and everyone involved in it.

Part 2

The performance will be marked out of a possible total of 45 marks. On the day of your examination on theatre in education it would be helpful to have the audience you planned for watching on that day. If for practical reasons this is not possible, do not worry; your moderator is highly experienced and will understand what you have been aiming to do. Whatever skill you present, you must show the examiner that your contribution:

■ is relevant to the style of the whole piece

■ demonstrates an understanding of period, society and culture in which the piece is set

■ demonstrates creativity and imagination

■ demonstrates awareness of the needs of your target audience.

6 Physical theatre

6.1

In this chapter you will learn to:

consider the development of physical theatre

consider what makes physical theatre different from other forms of theatre

prepare for and perform a piece of physical theatre

identify a target audience.

Key terms

Genre: style, type or family.

What is physical theatre?

Physical theatre is a **genre** or style of performance which makes use of the body as its primary means of performance and communication with the audience. It is a visual form of theatre where the actor concentrates on the use of the body, shape and position, facial expression, movement, gesture and posture.

Physical theatre focuses on the narrative, which is the telling of a story. The emphasis for the work you produce in this Controlled Assessment Option will be on drama, and should concentrate on relationships, characterisation, conflict and narrative.

Your audience must be carefully considered and you should ask yourself 'who is this drama for and what do I want my audience to get from this performance?' The consideration of your audience is crucial to the success of your project.

Your performance must have a definite form, with a beginning, a middle and an end, and the development of the piece should be easily identified as you progress.

A *A typically energetic Theatre de Complicite performance*

B *Harlequin character*

Activity

1   Research some theatre companies who specialise in physical theatre, for example, Theatre de Complicite or Kneehigh.

Styles of physical theatre

There are various styles of physical theatre including physical comedy, mime, contemporary dance, theatrical clowning and theatrical aerobatics.

Some companies only use physical theatre in their performances but many companies will use aspects of physical theatre as part of their performance outcomes.

The most famous development of this type of theatre came from the Lecoq School in Paris. Here students followed the method of Jaques Lecoq. His work developed from mask work, Commedia dell'Arte and his interest in physical theatre.

Skills study

Find out about the work of Jacques Lecoq.

kerboodle

In recent years a most popular company has developed using a pure form of physical theatre. This company has developed using the body, everyday objects, such as bin lids, brushes and spades, and percussion instruments to create a dynamic, exciting and energetic spectacle. This company is called 'Stomp'. The company have a touring show as well as a West End venue.

Skills study

Find out about Stomp and its latest performance.

C   *Physical theatre perfomed to its fullest by these performers from* **Stomp**

When exploring this aspect of performance, we must ask ourselves and the members of our group 'what are we trying to achieve from a performance perspective, and what do we want our audience to feel?'

⬭links

www.stomp.co.uk

Planning a performance

Before you begin your planning, you and your group must ask yourselves a number of questions:

- Do we have a suitable performance space?
- Where are we going to perform our project?
- What type of performance do we hope to achieve?

Physical theatre lends itself to producing a large performance on a grand scale. Think of the opening and closing ceremonies of a large-scale international event, such as the Olympic Games. This was physical theatre in the extreme sense with the **narrative** firmly identified and a **target audience** of the world!

D   *Street theatre involving lots of moving people*

6.2 Developing a performance

Your project will obviously be on a smaller scale, but a great deal of planning will have to be undertaken for it to be successful. The attention to detail you give to your initial planning is time well spent as the better prepared you are, the better use of time will be made. The **scenario** you and your group develop will help you with the structure of your performance and **stage form**.

If you decide to perform in a large performance space like a sports hall or an arena you will also have to ensure that you can rehearse in that same space as a change in location without rehearsing there can cause problems in performance terms.

Planning

You will need to plan a timetable of rehearsal time with the help of your stage manager to ensure rehearsals are well spent and time is not wasted. Your group will need a reasonable sense of rhythm, creativity and good movement skills. You will also be aware of **dynamics** and how live sound and recorded sound will be part of your performance planning. Other considerations include technical and design options that will be linked to your performance outcomes.

A *The* **Ella and the Ashes** *production by the Physical Theatre Group DV8*

Your performance

When considering where to begin from a performance perspective, you also need to be aware of the way your body movements can be integrated into your performance piece.

There are five basic body movements:

- stepping
- travelling
- turning
- jumping
- gesture.

These movements should be explored through a series of activities and exercises.

Stepping

Think of as many ways as you can of 'stepping'. There is stepping high on your toes, low on your toes, stepping taking wide strides, stepping taking small strides, stepping with your feet flat, stepping using the sides of your feet.

Take notes as you do these exercises to focus on how it feels to move in this way. Observe other members of your group as they try these movements.

Activity

1 Play 'follow my leader':

a Make a line of six people.

b The first person sets off around the room and walks in their normal way around the room; the five other members of the group observe.

c After the first circuit, the second person follows and copies exactly the way the person in front is walking but chooses one characteristic and slightly exaggerates it (the way the person swings their arms or the length of their stride).

d Each person then joins in turn, exaggerating a different aspect.

e Once the line is moving comfortably, and all have tried the walk of the leader, the leader joins the back of the line and the next person takes over as leader.

The exercise is repeated until everyone has had a turn as leader. It is an amazing feeling to try to walk in someone else's shoes! This is an excellent and fun warm-up exercise and, although simple in form, it emphasises that the way we walk immediately identifies the type of person we are.

B *The chorus line*

Travelling

How do we travel and, more importantly, how will you and your group members travel to ensure fluidity of movement in performance terms?

There are many ways we can travel around our performance space and these include rolling, jumping, sliding, or adding shape and form to our travels by, for example, adding cartwheels.

Turning

The way we turn and interact with each other defines the movement made. We can pivot or turn whilst travelling to add shape to the movement sequence.

C *Chinese Ballet Company.* **Swan Lake**, *Lowry Theatre Production*

Jumping

Another way to make movement around the performance space interesting is to add **jumps**. There are five basic jumps and these include: hopping, leaping onto one foot, leaping onto two feet, leaping from one foot to one foot and leaping from both feet and landing on both feet and hopscotch.

Gesture

Gesture is perhaps one of the most important aspects of performance work in physical theatre. Gesture includes functional movements of the body, waves, nods, arm movements and hand and facial expression. The use of the face, including the eyes, is particularly important in this type of performance.

We use gesture unconsciously in our everyday lives, from giving directions to emphasising our conversations. We must now use them in an exaggerated form to add to our physical theatre performance.

D *Children playing hopscotch*

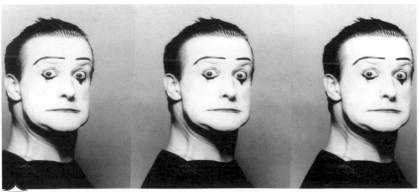

E *Mime artist Rowan Tolley*

Skills study

In Photo **D** the children are playing hopscotch. Find out about jumping games like this, or leapfrog for example. How could you use these movements in your physical piece?

Activity

2   Make a list of the different gestures you have used and observed in use in your everyday life.

There are many ways of starting your work on this project, but some simple exercises are a good introduction. The simplicity of the action and the visual outcomes of the repetition of the movement are where the power of the dramatic form lies.

3   Divide into pairs. Use a simple mirroring exercise to begin: combing your hair, brushing your teeth, putting on your make-up, or having a shave. Observe your partner and then try to copy the movement in every detail. Do this in slow motion first and then build up to normal speed. See if you can get to the point when the leader changes and the audience cannot see the changeover point.

Remember

Keep your ideas simple. The power is in the repetitive form.

Music and Sound

The choice of music and the sounds integrated into the performance are really important in this option and will be crucial to its success. This should be researched from the outset and form part of your early planning. You and you group should experiment with a variety of music and sounds. Are you using pre-recorded music or abstract sound or a combination of both? Another possible consideration is the creation of a 'soundscape' where abstract sounds and key words combine to produce your sound stimulus. This will help to underpin the narrative which links to the action you perform.

Remember

You must have a minimum of two performers, but your group can be large, as long as everyone's individual contribution is identified for assessment purposes.

F   *Theatre de Complicite in action*

For purposes of this Controlled Assessment task you and your group will work together to produce a physical theatre performance.

Case study

What makes a good citizen?

You can adapt the work in this case study to suit your group size. There will be four groups for performance purposes. The performance is linked to citizenship.

This project will enable you to explore a number of complex issues

through movement and narrative form. You will explore:

- a wide range of ethnic origins
- peer group pressure
- dangers to young people in today's society
- what young people perceive as dangerous.

The issue of 'citizenship' is universal in its appeal. It has now been acknowledged as so important that it forms part of the National Curriculum and must feature as part of the timetable in all schools. Why do you think this is the case? What has happened in our society to provoke this? These and other questions should form part of your planning once your group is established. Diagrams **A** and **B** will also give you some starter activities to explore before you begin. You should then ask yourselves what are your expectations of your performance piece and who is your target audience?

A Brainstorm the theme

When is our play set?

Who are the citizens in our play?

What are our expectations

A Good Citizen

Global issues?

How do our citizens live?

Role play

What is the power of our physical theatre style?

Study tip

You should ask yourselves about your audience and expectations for each Controlled Assessment Option you cover.

B   *Ideas to consider*

You will research and create a piece of physical theatre for performance to an audience. For the purpose of this case study, your target audience is upper school pupils and above. You must work in a group of not less than two.

For research and performance purposes you must now divide into groups. There must be four groups to represent the four 'societies' that are to be explored. The group sizes do not have to be the same. Each group will have a task: to build a base performance area. Each group will approach the task differently to emphasise the differences in their societies. There are four discrete groups representing four different societies through cultural, political and climatic differences.

Research

Society One: Communism

Think of colours, sounds and music to represent this society. The climate is warm. Work together as a team, number your leaders, all are equal although you must use a government to emphasise political belief. Communism involves the abolition of private property by a revolutionary movement. The responsibility for the people is vested in the State.

Society Two: Spiritualism

Think of colours, sounds and music to represent this society. The climate is humid. There is a natural order. Spirit Nation does not necessarily have a political belief. Many find their way through method. For purposes of our project, there is an existence called the 'Spirit World'. The Spirit World exists in the same space that the earth plane does, and is all around you.

Communism	Spiritualism
	All performers in one tight group at opening of performance	
Anarchy	Hierarchy

D   *Performance in the round: layout*

Society Three: Hierarchy

Think of colours, sounds and music to represent this society. The climate is cold. There is a single dictator who orders the masses to do their bidding. A dictatorship is a form of government with absolute power.

Society Four: Anarchy

Think of colours, sounds and music to represent this society. The climate is hot. There is no leader and no followers. There is no sense of community, and nothing gets done. This society maximises the individual's liberty and social equality.

C   *A poster from the Communist USSR*

Study tip

The process of planning and creating your performance gains 15 marks. You are judged on how well you work within the group and how well you evaluate the process.

Activity

1   Once you have decided on your group, research examples of your society. Explore how you will represent this in performance.

E   *Anarchy is a theory that proposes a state without government or law*

6.4   Option 6: Set design

The technical and design options will be accommodated with two options explored through each of the societies. For example, 'Communism' will explore Set design and Masks. The process for study, however, will be transferable to any of the design and technical options.

You are required to create a scale model of the set, to include drawings, methods of building, set changes and health and safety issues. You will design a set for one of the performance communities to feature as part of the performance as a whole. Your set design will be for a performance in the round. The audience will sit all around the performance area.

As your audience enters, some performers will be sitting in the actual audience space. How will this affect the audience? How will they react to this? Are you having enough chairs for all your audience to be seated? If not, how will they react?

A   *Royal Exchange Theatre, Manchester*

There are a number of considerations when designing a set for a physical theatre performance. The most important aspects include 'can the audience see?' and 'is there enough room for your performers?' Your set will need to display a number of **symbolic** items so your audience can easily identify the type of society represented.

Remember that the Communist system would restrain its citizens, by force if necessary. How would you integrate these ideas into your design? Carefully consider signage and performers' involvement. What colours would you associate with this community and why?

Key terms

Symbolic: referring to a sign or thing representing or typifying something.

Study tip

Although you are exploring Communism for your set design, the skills you are exploring are transferable to all the other societies.

Activity

1   What symbols or designs would identify the Communist society? What symbols or shapes would the audience recognise in advance? How could you show this in your design?

6.5 Option 7: Costume design

As a costume designer for a piece of physical theatre your first concern must address the question 'can the actors move well without being restricted by their costume?' Costume will always have a big impact on the performer and the audience and the impact is often considerable.

For this case study you will design a costume for a member of the **Spiritualist Society.**

The Spirit World is a place represented in many plays and stories. It is a world which exists in the same space as the earth plane, but must look different to the other societies of the earth plane. Remember that the process of costume design for the Spiritualist world is transferable to the other communities. To help you to explore this world, imagine you are standing in a fog. The fog is all around you. Everything else that is normally around you is there also, whether you see it through the fog or not. Where does the 'fog' stop and everything else begin? In this way the Spirit World exists in the same space as the earth plane exists.

The Spiritualist Society shows natural order with the world and natural order with its surroundings. Remember, your actors have to have a great deal of freedom to move as the narrative will be told through physical means.

As costume designer you will have to research a variety of fabrics which enable your actors that degree of freedom. You should consider: are you setting your Spiritualist society in a particular time and place?; and how will this be reflected in your design? Your preliminary drawings will be very important as they will link the style of the performance to the society you are exploring. Remember to consider colours carefully and how they will be altered under stage lights. Your costume must be used in rehearsals and tested in this way, so you have no nasty shocks once other design elements are added in performance terms.

How would you show to the audience that your actors are not of this world? What techniques can you explore and employ to show this?

Skills study

- use of space in relation to the actors and the audience
- use of textures, colours and fabrics, material and techniques.

A *Researching costume design is integral to your production*

6.6   Option 8: Make-up

For the purpose of this case study, the make-up will be for the Hierarchy society. The use of make-up in a piece of physical theatre demands a great deal from the designer. The audience is in the round and therefore positioned close to the performers. The actors will be moving around the stage and physical activity will cause them to get hot, particularly under the stage lights. This has to be carefully considered by the make-up designer.

An interesting technique to consider would be to make up half the actor's face in a fantasy design and half the face naturalistic.

The designer must practise the application of the make-up on the actor and then allow them to use it during the rehearsal process. The physical aspect of the production may have a direct effect on the type of make-up used, and this will have to be carefully explored.

You must produce two contrasting make-ups for assessment purposes. Consider how you creatively can achieve it.

A   *An example of the hard work and effort that goes into fantasy make-up*

6.7 Option 9: Properties

The society to consider for purposes of the case study is 'Anarchy, the no-government system of socialism'. Properties are to be used with great care and consideration for physical theatre purposes. They can be used as symbols of the community to be explored. For assessment purposes you must design and manufacture two different stage properties for Anarchy.

A *Stomp using their stage props*

Stomp use everyday objects in their performances including dustbins, bin lids, bushes, brooms, cans, etc. to create soundscapes and rhythm for the actors to move to.

The properties you design will represent the ideals of the Anarchist structures of society, and your research will assist you.

Activity

1   a   Join in the group discussion about the types of movement that will represent the Anarchist society.

     b   Draw up a props list, taking into account how heavy the props are and how the performers must move with them.

     c   Consider whether the props can be used to represent more than one thing. How will the performers make it clear that the representation has changed?

6.8 Option 10: Masks

For purposes of the case study the society you will explore is 'Communism'. Mask work and mask design is probably the one area of study best suited to the physical theatre option. The narrative of the performance is communicated to the audience through movement, gesture and mime and the performers are for the most part not relying on speech to communicate the storyline to their audience.

Your mask design therefore can happily involve the whole face, or even the whole head! You have to consider that your actor has to be able to see, and the mask must be comfortable to wear in performance terms.

As your Communist state demands uniformity of vision, all your masks could be exactly the same in every detail. This society demands equal sharing of all work, according to ability. For your second contrasting mask design you could therefore design a mask to represent the State. The audience would instantly recognise the difference and a dramatic moment would occur. The responsibility for the public need is vested in the State.

Your mask can be used as a theatrical tool to help provide the performers with the narrative.

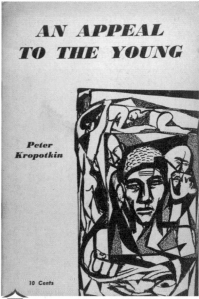

A A revolutionary pamphlet by Peter Kropotkin

B Masks are well-suited to physical theatre

6.9 Option 11: Puppets

Many theatre companies use huge puppets to represent the characters in their productions. Larger-than-life puppets with larger-than-life characteristics are used as a visual stimulus on the stage.

A   *Kneehigh Touring Theatre Puppet*

For purposes of the case study the Spiritualist Society will be considered here. This society would give great opportunity for the puppet designer. Physical theatre relies on visual stimulus and movement rather than speech, so this would allow the construction of huge puppets to be considered. The methods of construction of the puppet would have to be carefully considered as your puppet would have to be able to move freely round the stage, but this could form part of the interpretation of this interesting society. Perhaps your puppet could be a representative of the Spirit World as spirits try to communicate with our world.

6.10 Option 12: Lighting

The fantasy element of this case study would give a great deal of opportunity to the lighting designer. The lighting of the performance areas would be clearly linked to the theme of the performance with identifiable colours representing the habitats of the different societies of Communism, Spiritualism, Hierarchy and Anarchy. Careful research and group discussion could decide these representative colours.

You must show an exploration of the lights available to you and what effects you can create on your performance space. Consider also the use of **gobos** to represent the different cultures explored and represented in performance.

Key terms

Gobo: Small metal plate inserted behind spotlight to project a chosen image onto the stage.

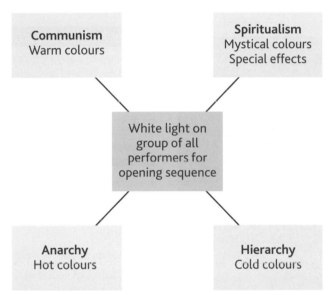

```
Communism          Spiritualism
Warm colours       Mystical colours
                   Special effects

        White light on
        group of all
        performers for
        opening sequence

Anarchy            Hierarchy
Hot colours        Cold colours
```

A *Lighting design for opening sequence*

B *Lighting can create ghostly effects …*

C *… and add dramatic emphasis*

6.11 Option 13: Sound

Of all the design elements the sound designer has a really challenging and exciting role in the production of a piece of physical theatre for performance. For purposes of this case study the sound designer has to consider all four societies and how to bring them together as a whole, to link the performances and create the 'Sound Narrative'.

Your working plot must be detailed and accurate, and careful rehearsal of the sound will be necessary for a successful outcome to the whole performance. The soundscape that you choose must represent the four societies in the performance, and detailed cuing will be vital to the success of the performance.

Create soundscapes for each of the four societies and bring them together as a whole.

A *A sound desk*

Study tip

Be aware of copyright restrictions on all music and recordings. How will this apply to your performance?

Skills study

- awareness of the significance of sound in performance
- use of live/recorded sound effects
- ability to record, mix and edit
- control of sound at appropriate levels for background of dramatic effect.

6.12 Option 14: Stage management

The successful stage manager must be organised and authoritative, and for the purposes of managing a piece of physical theatre this will be crucial.

As stage manager you are responsible for the organisation and control of all aspects of the performance: backstage, onstage and during and after the performance.

This citizenship project is complex in form and structure, and will require a good stage manager to bring the performance together. Your skills will be adequately tested here.

You will need:

- a detailed copy of the scenario
- evidence of health and safety factors
- rehearsal schedules
- to prepare the areas for rehearsals and performance
- to plan how you will run the show
- to consider your performers and audience.

You will also need to manage all aspects of the performance from a technical and design perspective. Another thing you will have to consider in managing this project is how to successfully manage the four different societies and give equal time for rehearsal and use of the performance space. You will need to be seen to be fair when making your decisions.

You must create a detailed plan of the set, with the four society areas clearly marked out in performance terms.

You should also create a detailed prompt copy of the scenario of the performance.

Experiment during the rehearsal stage with the performers and your technicians and designers. You must also have a good working knowledge of all technical aspects of the production, but this will be your designer's responsibility. You will only oversee the organisation and be responsible for managing the team.

A *A carefully stage-managed performance*

Keep the performance area clearly marked and decide what needs to come on and off and where it goes, who will bring things on and off, and who will strike. There is nothing worse in any performance than a piece of furniture being left on the stage when it should have been removed. It is often a chair!

Lastly you must consider the 'flow' of the performance piece. Physical theatre demands controlled movement by your actors, and you will be responsible for managing them. Good luck!

Study tip

Manage your time wisely.

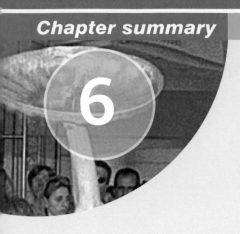

The work you do on this Controlled Assessment task will be useful in all elements of this course. Your practical skills will be relevant to all other practical tasks, and you will be able to analyse them and write about them on the written paper.

Unit 1: The written paper

The Controlled Assessment task Physical theatre is ideal for answering Section A questions. You may be able to give details of your stimulus or starting point and why this theme was chosen. You may also be able to explain how you developed the ideas into a piece of drama.

As you rehearsed your work you will have made improvements and changes, and you may be asked to say how these were done and why – and whether they made the work more successful. There may be the opportunity to analyse the strengths and weaknesses of the whole piece or of your own personal skills.

You will be able to show your understanding of different performance styles and why you chose different styles in your work. You will be able to explain your own contribution to the work.

You can see that it is therefore very important to keep a record of the work you have done. You may do this as a diary, as a series of recordings or as photographs. You could make videos of rehearsals, which will also help you to refine your work. Make sure that you have a video of your final performance as this will be great when you come to revise for the written paper.

Design and technical students will have a detailed record of their progress as part of their practical assessment, and this will be an excellent revision tool too.

If you answer this question there will be 40 marks available, and that is half of the marks for the whole paper, so you will have to make sure that you revise the work thoroughly so that you can give plenty of detail.

You will be able to use clearly labelled sketches and diagrams in your answer, so practise these in your revision period.

You will have 45 minutes to write your answer.

Unit 2: The Controlled Assessment task

When you have finished this work, you will perform it in front of an audience. This could be the rest of your group, friends and relatives, a school assembly or the public. A moderator may be present and their job is to moderate the marking of your teacher.

All the way through your rehearsal period you should ask for feedback. Someone in your group not involved in a particular scene or section can watch and comment on your work and suggest improvements, as could someone from another group. You can also make videos of your work in progress.

Your teacher will be awarding you a mark for your preparation, so his or her feedback will be very important. You should show an awareness

Study tip

You may have used a live performance you have seen to inspire this work, so do not forget to revise this if you want to answer a Section C question.

of how you can develop your work, and you should be able to work co-operatively and creatively in the group.

In your final performance, you will be assessed on how you use your practical skills to put your ideas across to the audience. In physical theatre, you will be able to show a variety of skills. Make sure that you choose skills which will help to show your ability. If, for example, you enjoy working with a script, then be sure to be involved in those scenes or sections. If you are a talented dancer, take responsibility for this aspect of the work.

Your teacher will be crediting:

- your creative approach
- originality
- how you relate text and different styles
- how you sustain the quality of your performance
- your use of voice, movement, gesture, facial expression and how you relate to others on stage.

If you are fully prepared, you will really enjoy your performance, and so will your audience.

7.1 Thinking about the skills you have developed

In this chapter you will learn:

what the written paper involves

how to prepare yourself for it.

■ What's the point of the written paper?

This is your opportunity to think back over all the practical work you have done and seen during your course, and demonstrate to an examiner what you have done and what you have learnt.

Drama is a practical activity, and you need to show that you have understood what you were doing in your practical work and also show you can analyse and evaluate your work and that of others. You will need to be able to use the terminology you have learnt as a performer, a designer or a technician.

■ What is in the written paper?

There are three sections, offering a total of five questions.

You **must** answer Section A and then choose **one** question from either of the other sections:

- Section A: Question 1 is on practical work completed during your course, and is compulsory.
- Section B: Questions 2 and 3 are about your study and performance of a scripted play.
- Section C: Questions 4 and 5 are about your study of a live theatre production seen as part of your course.

You will have 1½ hours to complete your answers. Each question is worth 40 marks. The total is out of 80.

■ Thinking about the skills you have developed

Throughout this book, in all the options, you have been advised to keep a detailed record of the work you have done. You may have a diary, sound recordings, photographs and videos. You will also have a script or scenario document which probably has lots of notes written on it.

Design and technical students will have detailed records of what they have done. They may have sketches and lists they created to work from for the performance.

Make a list of the skills you have used during your preparation period.

Think and write notes about how good you were with these skills before you started GCSE Drama and how good you are now.

Are there specific moments or events in the preparation or performance that helped you to improve more than others?

■ Preparing for the written paper

- Re-read all the information you have gathered during the preparation time and performance.
- Decide on the specific pieces of practical work you can best write about for Section A.
- Decide whether you will tackle a question in Section B or Section C.
- Look at this chapter to see what you need to write for each part of Section A and Section B or Section C. Make notes about your work that answer those question parts.
- Tackle the practice questions on pages 152–4 as if you were in an examination.

Section A: Practical work completed during the course

For Question 1 you can write about any practical work you have done as part of the course as an actor, a designer or a technician. As with the controlled assessments you will have done, this work could be scripted, devised, improvised, physical theatre or theatre-in-education work, and the focus of the questions will always be on the personal skills you have developed during the preparation and performance of the selected piece of work.

You must answer all four parts of Question 1 (01, 02, 03 and 04) and you must focus on the same piece of performance work, using the same contribution as actor, designer or technician. Each part is worth 10 marks. If you feel that sketches or diagrams would give your answer more clarity then you can include them in any of your answers to these questions, however these should be used to illustrate a point not replace the written version.

■ Question 01: Description of a piece of practical work that you completed during the course

Question 01 is your opportunity to tell the examiner what the piece was about and what your contribution to it was. You will need to include all of the following points:

- A brief description of the piece, which should not need to be more than a couple of sentences in length to answer the question, 'What was the piece about?'
- A statement on the period in which it was set.
- A statement on the genre of the piece; what kind of drama is it? What category would you put the piece in if it was in a DVD library? Typical genres are tragedy, comedy, horror, melodrama but you might decide that the genre is best identified as theatre-in-education, verbatim theatre or theatre of cruelty.
- A statement on the style adopted by your group in the performance of the piece: for example, naturalistic, physical, Brechtian or absurdist.
- A statement on the performance space used; this should give some identification of the positioning of your audience so, in order to be clear, you should use terms like proscenium arch (end on), traverse, thrust or apron staging.
- A statement on your target audience; even if you only performed it to the rest of your class you should tell the examiner that, in this case, it was performed to your teacher and your peers.
- A statement on your contribution to the piece; this need only be a statement that tells the examiner that you were an actor or the costume designer or the lighting technician. You must only state one contribution (as actor, designer or technician) in the same way that you can only contribute one option to your practical work and it will be this same contribution, stated here, that you will use for the rest of Section A.

Study tip

As you work on your practical options, think ahead about the questions you will be asked in the written paper. Building them into your planning will make it easier for you to remember and answer them later.

Remember

Although all four questions in Section A are worth 10 marks each, the first (01) need not take as much time and space as the following three parts.

Study tip

Every time you prepare for a practical project, make detailed notes on your choice of theme or play, the style you decided upon, your performance space and the equipment you may have worked with. Always make sure that you are able to make notes of how and reasons why you worked as you did.

- If you have performed using technical and design support then give the examiner a flavour of this, but only if it will make your response clearer. If you did not have technical and design support you need not mention this; it is only to help the examiner understand the kind of piece it was that you performed.

Each time you start a new piece of practical work, you should write down your thoughts on these areas, then update them in the middle of the rehearsal period and once again after the piece is completed. This will provide excellent preparation for answering Question 01 in your exam.

■ Question 02: Explanation of your own contribution

Question 02 asks you to explain what you did. This must relate to the contribution that you identified in 01. Examiners will look for you to explain the skills that you used in the piece:

Acting

- An understanding of the character that you played and how your characterisation was created for the role through, for example, your way of talking, your way of walking, your specific movements, gestures and facial expressions.
- An indication of the choices that you made in your selection of these characteristics, including the application of necessary acting skills.
- An indication of the age and status of your character and the other demands of the role: for example, the selection of an appropriate accent.

Design

- An understanding of your chosen area of design through an explanation of, for example, materials, scale, proportion, construction.
- An application of the skills you personally used and applied to this piece of practical work through considerations of, for example colour, fabrics, selected staging.
- An indication of the context for your choices through references to, for example, text, style or genre.

Technical

- An understanding of your chosen area of technical work through an explanation of, for example, lights (lanterns, intensity) or sound (amplification, cuing).
- An application of the skills you personally used and applied to this piece of practical work through considerations of, for example, specific effects, colour, direction, angles, intensity, music, volume.
- An indication of the context for your choices through references to, for example, text, style or genre.

Always bear in mind that the examiners do not know you or what you did. In your written paper, you need to demonstrate that you knew what you were doing and understood the skills that you applied in this piece of practical work.

Choose any piece of practical work you have recently done or are preparing.

■ On a large sheet of paper, list the bullet points under Question 01.

■ Fill in the details next to each point. Some answers will be easy, others such as style or genre may need some discussion. If you are working on a Controlled Assessment piece, you will now have a useful guide for revision.

■ Now try the same exercise with the bullet points for Question 02. You may need to talk through some of your answers with your teacher or with the others in your group.

Congratulations! You should now be able answer half of Section A.

A *Elinor at the first day read through of* **Twelfth Night** *at the Orange Tree Theatre, Richmond*

■ Question 03: Analysis of your own preparation

In **Question 03**, you will need to write about the preparation of your own work during the rehearsal stage. The examiner will want to know how you worked, what methods you used and why you used them. You will need to consider, for example:

■ The needs of the production. You will need to show awareness of the need for changes, for example, to establish period, place or mood through pace, use of special effects, live sound, costume, set and properties.

■ Problems encountered in performance, design or technical aspects. You might consider the way you worked together with the other members of your group on one specific moment for a particular effect. You should focus on how your ideas changed as you experimented with different approaches to the problems.

■ As performers you will need to consider, for example, the specific exercises you selected, why they were appropriate and how they solved a problem during the rehearsals. The physical difficulties encountered and specific effects you included like developing the synchronised sections of the performed piece.

■ As designers or technicians, you should consider the way your ideas were affected by factors like budgetary constraints, performers' abilities or health and safety issues.

Remember

Question 01 requires that you make a number of statements that do not need to be further explained, but all of the other questions should be answered with reasons given for the points you make. For Questions 02, 03 and 04, you should give a reason to justify your suggestion. For example, 'I whispered the line because I needed to show that I was afraid of being heard'.

Question 04: Evaluation of your own contribution to the work

Question 04 will ask you to evaluate your contribution to the work you have written about in this section, which means that you will have to make a judgement on how effective or successful you thought it was.

You will need to show awareness of, for example:

- Your own skills as demonstrated in particular moments of the performance. These moments should be fully identified so that you can show how your skills were applied.
- Your strengths and weaknesses in the performance in terms of, for example, characterisation, projection, effectiveness and appropriateness of design or technical work undertaken.
- The way the audience appeared to respond to your work in terms of spontaneous emotion, or laughter, or in post-performance feedback.

B *Orange Tree Theatre's* **Twelfth Night** *company in read through*

You should focus on your own skills throughout this response and, where you feel some discussion of your group members appears appropriate, you should ensure that your contribution has clear prominence. This is true of all responses in Section A.

What about me? I am a stage manager

The stage manager has one of the most important roles, and yet is nearly always forgotten, especially when they do a good job. For the purposes of GCSE Drama, your work fits in somewhere between design and technical aspects, since you will have to know how every piece fits together for the final performance and make sure that it does so. You will probably have more working notes than anyone else in the group, and will have been part of the discussions. While this is a strength, it can also be a problem.

If you choose to answer a question from the point of view of stage manager, be careful. Your revision aim will be to condense your notes so that the focus is on your own contribution. Break down the process into clear stages. Check against the bullet points for relevant material to include in your answer.

> **Study tip**
> - Gather your answers while you are working on your Controlled Assessment.
> - Do a bit at a time rather than attempt to record everything at the end.
> - Always make clear notes of HOW and WHY things were done.

C *The stage manager is integral to the smooth direction of a production*

Section B: Study and performance of a scripted play

■ Is there a choice of question?

You will be given a choice of two questions, Question 2 (05, 06) or Question 3 (07, 08). Always answer on work that is most familiar to you and where you can make the most number of points.

There will be an opportunity for you to write about performing, design or technical aspects. Each part of the question is worth 20 marks. They have equal marks, so you need to spend equal time and effort on each part:

- 05 and 07 will ask you to describe or explain what you did.
- 06 and 08 will ask you to analyse or evaluate the success of your work.

Although you will be asked to focus on a particular scene or section that you have performed during your course, you should have an understanding of the whole play. This means that you must be prepared to write in detail about the playwright's intentions and your interpretation of the script, with examples to support your answer.

■ Questions about your performance

05, 07: Description or explanation of what you did

As a performer, you will have had to interpret a character and find ways of communicating that character on stage. For this question you should use a script that you have performed and that you are able to write about with enthusiasm and detail.

When approaching any script you will need to think about:

- The playwright's intentions.
  - What has the playwright said about this play, perhaps in their introduction to the play script, or in interviews found during your research?
  - Which genre and period was the playwright writing within?
  - What did you find out about your character from their lines, or from what other characters say about them?
  - What did you find out about your character from the stage directions?
- Your interpretation.
  - What style did you decide to use for this play? Was it as the playwright suggested or did you take a different, perhaps more physical, approach?
  - How did you act in order to communicate the character's age, status, mannerisms?
  - How were relationships with other characters communicated on stage? How did you use eye contact, physical contact and use of space to show what your character feels or thinks about others on stage?

- Your performance skills.
    - Voice: What accent, pitch, tone, and emphasis did you find most appropriate? When were they used in the scene or section?
    - Movement: What kinds of gesture, posture or physical theatre skills did you use to make the character convincing to an audience?
    - Facial expression: What changes of facial expression did you use to communicate the character's changes of mood?
    - How were your skills developed during the rehearsal period?

A *Orange Tree Theatre's* **Twelfth Night** *company in dress rehearsal*

06, 08: Analysis or evaluation of what you did

The second part of these questions is about analysis or evaluation. You will need to make judgements on the quality of your work with details from the performance of the scene or section.

When you have performed your scripted play, you will need to think about, and make notes on, the following points:

- Your own strengths and weaknesses in performing your character. Perhaps your role involved the use of expressive gestures or facial expressions at particular moments that you can evaluate clearly.
- Strengths and weaknesses of other members of your group in performance. How did they affect your performance for better or perhaps for worse?
- Awareness of genre, style or period. Which moments of the performance demonstrated your success in any of these areas?

- Moments of interaction between characters. How were these moments acted by you?
- Pace and pause. When was either of these particularly successful in building excitement, creating tension or emphasising a point?

Most importantly for this answer, you should focus on the success of your own performance.

- With what moment of performance can you demonstrate your level of success? Why do you think that any moment you include in your answer was a moment of success, or perhaps a relative failure?

B *Orange Tree Theatre's* **Twelfth Night** *company in rehearsal*

Design and technical questions

05, 07: Description or explanation of what you did

As with performers, if you are a designer or a technician, you need to select the play for use in this question very carefully. In this section, you will always be credited for sharing your enthusiasm for the design or technical work that you did on a scripted play.

As you begin work on any play, you will share some of the preparation aspects undertaken by performers:

- You should consider the playwright's intentions:
  - What the playwright said about this play, together with the genre and period within which the playwright was writing.
  - What in the script gave you your first design or technical ideas?
  - What were the main demands or challenges in the script for your role as designer or technician?
  - If you were engaged as a stage manager, how did you take account of what was required of you from reading the script?

- You should also consider your own intentions, and those of your group:
  - What was the style that you decided to use? How much was original, and decided by you, and how much did you use influences from others?
  - What scale was the performance to be; a workshop performance or perhaps a grand evening performance?
  - Who were the target audience? How did you intend to affect them?
- Most importantly you should describe and explain your own specific skills in terms of design or technical options.

Design options

- Costumes: you will have to discuss fabrics, textures, colours along with details and reasons for their choice.
- Set: discuss the way you used space and levels as well the way you represented location by flats, projection, materials, colours and textures.
- Make-up, masks or puppets: you will need to discuss these in terms of style, proportion, colours and appropriateness.
- Awareness of health and safety factors: each option has its own set of health and safety factors such as fireproofing, checking for allergies or securing loose cables; be fully aware of these.

For all design options, it is important to show some integration of design elements into overall design concepts. This demonstrates to the examiner that you did your job properly and consulted with others when choosing colours or images appropriate to the mood or atmosphere and ensuring consistency between costume and set.

Technical options

- Lighting: discuss your use of colours, intensity, plot and special effects such as gobos, projection of digital images.
- Sound: refer to whether it was live, recorded or a mix of both. Refer to the need for balance and the equipment you used.
- Properties: refer to how they were used and managed (whether personal or stage props) and how they contributed to the production.
- Awareness of health and safety factors: refer to taping cables, use of fire extinguishers and the potential hazards of using electrical equipment.

Every part of a production has to fit together, and it is important to show some integration of elements into overall design concepts. You will need to show that you have thought about the choice of sound effects or levels appropriate to the mood of the scene and consistent with the visual effects of set and costume.

C   *HumDrum production of* James & the Giant Peach

A checklist: what do I need to do to achieve high marks in Section B Study and performance of a scripted play?

- Identify the play upon which you are focusing, giving the playwright's name.

- Select an appropriate extract – the question will not ask you about the complete play, so make sure you choose a scene or section that gives you plenty of scope to write at length.

- The clarity of your work is most important; if your response is very clear, it should reach the top band as long as you:

  - refer appropriately and purposefully to both the script and the practical work that you did with it

  - analyse and evaluate clearly your contribution, with some recognition of your strengths and weaknesses

- consider the contributions of others in the group and how this affected your contribution

- consider the impact of your own performance on your audience by reference to the way they responded

- consider the use of sketches, ground plans and diagrams, where any of these might illustrate the points that you wish to make.

■ In order to gain high marks you will have to:

- be very clear in everything that you say

- use references to the script and to the performance in a purposeful way, chosen by you to demonstrate your knowledge and understanding

- justify your statements fully and in detail.

D *Malvolio from* **Twelfth Night** *in his yellow stockings with Year 7 students in an Orange Tree Theatre workshop*

Section C: Study of a live theatre production seen

■ Which production should I write about?

As part of your course, it is always useful to visit live theatre productions, as these will influence how you do your own practical work. You can also write about one of these visits in Section C of the exam. The performance you write about must be one that you have studied as part of the course. In order to gain high marks, you must spend some time studying how the production actually worked, and how it managed to make an impact on you as a member of the audience. The marks awarded are the same as those given for Section B, where you write about a scripted play that you performed, so it is sensible to spend a similar amount of time in preparation for these questions in Section C.

■ In what way is Section C different from other sections?

The main difference is that you will have to write about a production you have seen as a member of an audience rather than as a participant. You will probably just see the production once, so you will have only a short time in which to absorb all the fine details. You may be so moved by the production that your head is full of images and sounds and emotions, and you find it difficult to say anything. If that is the case, relax, it will all fall into place eventually. Some people simply do not want to discuss a play on the way home.

■ How can I prepare for writing on a production that I've not been in?

Chapter 1 tells you that every single practical lesson prepares you for the written paper, as you gradually learn new vocabulary and skills and how to apply them. Very soon you will have absorbed enough knowledge to be able to comment in an informed way on other people's work. This book suggests that you do this as part of your practical work as you offer comments on each other.

One of the best ways of learning is to see professionals working and to observe the ways in which they tackle different aspects of the job. As a drama student, going to see live theatre works on two levels: you are there as a student to learn and you are also there as a member of an audience to be moved and entertained. The second is always the more important, because through it you will be able to feel how effective the production was. The knowledge you bring to it as a drama student will help you to understand just how and why the production worked.

Before the live theatre visit

It is important that you know the kind of performance that you are going to see. A readthrough of the script beforehand, if it is available, will make you aware of the demands of the performance, and perhaps give you an opinion on the characters or the design implications for the location. This foreknowledge will help you to focus on how it is to be performed, rather than just what happens in the story. If the script is not available, or you wish to keep some of the action as a surprise, then it is important to identify and understand the genre (the type of performance) of the play, or the style in which it is to be performed. A good idea is to do some workshop activities in advance of seeing the play, using research material that you have gleaned about the script or the company.

Look for the potential in the script, genre or style and refer to your knowledge and understanding of practical skills to see how the production applies these aspects.

At the theatre

Enjoy the experience of being a member of the audience. That's what the show is there for. By all means make notes, but please do not use lights of any kind. Actors hate it and fellow audience members are not too keen either. Write your notes in the interval. Draw sketches of set or costumes if you are able and make brief notes of colour, textures, lighting. Share what you have noticed with others in the intervals and on the way home. Enjoy the impact of the production and ask yourself the questions 'How?' and 'Why?' afterwards.

Don't expect to remember it all at once; details will come back later, especially when you have talked about it with others.

After the visit

Discuss the performance with your friends and your teachers afterwards, but always try to form your own personal opinion. There are no right or wrong answers here, as it is obviously a matter of personal taste what one member of the audience thought was effective and what another found tedious. It is this personal opinion that will help you gain the highest of marks, but you will need to be able to back up your views with clearly expressed reasons, and examples from the performance. It may be helpful to do further workshop activities in a group to try out some of the performance ideas you noticed in the production. Knowing how difficult it is to use a particular technique can increase your admiration for the members of the company who successfully used it in the performance that you saw.

■ Design and technical options

Preparing for design answers

It is always helpful to start by making sketches of the set and costumes. As designers, you should be able to do this when you visit the theatre. Sometimes the main set is on view at the start of the production or is left during the interval. This will make your task easier. Otherwise, you will have to rely on rapid sketches from memory in the interval or afterwards. You may be able to piece together a drawing from photographs in the programme, publicity material or in newspapers. The main thing is to have a visual image and some notes on colours, textures and materials.

A   *An actress performing in* **King Lear** *with Year 7 students in an Orange Tree Theatre workshop*

Activity

1 Set design

a By yourself:

On an A3 sheet, write the title of the production.

In the centre draw a sketch of the set – it doesn't have to be a masterpiece. Add the main colours, in labels if easiest.

Around the sides of the sheet write down all the bullet points set out below.

Each member of the group should annotate the drawing, referring to as many bullet points as possible. (You could maybe make photocopies for each student and one extra as a main copy for the whole class.)

Colour-code your comments – use separate colours for What? How? and Why?

b As a group:

Ask the other members of your group to describe the set as if taking a mental walk around it. Remember to follow a set pattern, for example, from downstage left in a curve to downstage right. Use the correct stage positioning. If you are unsure, look at page 85 in Chapter 4.

This will help everyone get into the habit of organising their thoughts and ideas by giving a simple structure. Get into the habit of doing this by applying it to every set you use so that you can memorise them more easily.

- General impact and first impressions of the set.
- Description of the set following a clear and well-considered path round it. If you use correct terms, anyone should be able to follow your description.
- On the sheet fill in any details such as:
  - Period/Location: where is it set? When? How does the designer show this?
  - Structure: What form does it take? Why?
  - Levels: What levels are used? How? Why?
  - What illusion is the designer trying to create?
  - What materials do you think the designer chose to create that illusion?

You can adapt this exercise for other design options. When it is completed you can make notes and use the main sheet as a revision poster – pin it up where you can glance at it every day and be reminded. Add points as you remember them.

Period: 1914–1918
Shown by: Oil-lamps and candles for lighting, props-e.g. steel helmets, mess tins costumes – authentic uniforms.

Door to the kitchen area

Location: A dug-out in the front-line trenches.
Shown by:

levels – steps leading up to surface

textures – rough timber, corrugated iron sheeting, timbers to support the roof

colours – earth coloured browns, muddy, drab

furniture – camp beds, folding chair for C.O. only, boxes for the others

Style: Naturalistic – it made you feel as if you were looking into a real trench dug-out. The accurate detail of costumes and the use of paraffin lamps and candles helped create an enclosed and cramped atmosphere. Ammunition boxes for seats and rough camp beds made it look like a place for working rather than comfort.

Entrance from surface

Genre: Anti-war drama, tragedy

B *Set design sheet in progress – details can be added as you think of them*

Preparing for answers about lighting and sound

These areas are more difficult to study in a live production from an entirely practical point of view, as you probably will not have the facilities in your centre to try and reproduce what you saw and heard in the theatre. You will, however, have most likely joined others in your group on the two exercises already described and will have a good idea as to how the performances worked alongside the sets and costumes to create particular effects.

Study tip

Although a good production will combine design and technical aspects, you need to select one upon which to focus. To score a high mark, you should have technical knowledge of the design or technical area you choose, preferably with practical experience of your own.

C   *The lighting at the King's Theatre, Southsea*

You can draw on your knowledge and understanding of practical skills to explain just how the lighting and sound helped take the atmosphere and mood on stage a notch higher. Many hundreds of students have seen productions of *The Woman in Black,* either in London or on tour, which presents an excellent example of lighting and sound being used together for dramatic effect.

■ What do I need to do to achieve high marks in the examination?

In order to gain marks in Band 1 (17–20), you will need to satisfy the examiner that your answers fit the description in the mark scheme for a Band 1 response. These mark bands always include the wording of the question to which they refer, so it is most important that you look carefully at the question that has been asked of you, and not one that you hoped or imagined to be there. Failure to focus appropriately on the question that has been set for you will be the most obvious limitation to your success. Key phrases are included in the mark bands to identify into which band your response should be placed, and answers in Band 1 are required to be 'very clear' with 'purposeful' references to the work you have done.

So, in order to succeed with your answers:

■ Always read the question. Look for words that appear in the question and reflect them in your response. If a question in Section B asks you to consider your 'aims' in producing a piece of work, then use that word in your response: for example, 'one of my aims in performing this role was to develop my acting skills'. Similarly, if the question refers to 'strengths and weaknesses', then you must focus on this aspect in your response. You can see that 'aims' and 'strengths and weaknesses' are not the same thing, and that your answer may be much less effective if you do not keep to the focus of how the question has been worded.

■ Be 'very clear'. The examiners will mark your responses with regard to your clarity, so you will need to ensure that you include enough practical detail, and that you produce your answers in a logical, well-organised style.

■ Provide 'purposeful' references to the work. A purposeful reference is one that is carefully selected to best support the statements that you make, rather than one that you use just because you learnt it especially for the exam.

■ Keep the focus on practical skills. This is a drama exam, so too much emphasis on the story, or on social interaction with your group members, is not going to score as well as a response that focuses on the drama skills required for your chosen performance.

■ Where you use sketches or diagrams, be sure to include clear annotations, remembering that these must not replace a written version.

■ Remember, it is your own personal, informed views that are required, so collect clear, practical evidence to justify your opinions.

What does the exam paper look like?

Here are the questions that were used in the 2011 exam with some helpful tips.

Section A: Practical work completed as part of the course

Practice questions

Question 1 Choose a piece of practical work in which you were involved as actor **or** designer **or** technician.

> **Study tip** The first sentence is called a 'leader', because it leads you into the question and tells you what you need to focus on. In this case, it asks you to pick a piece of practical work that you have worked on. You can base this Section A on any of the options.

01 Describe what the piece was about; state the style, period and genre of the piece, the performance space and any technical or design elements used and your target audience. You should state whether your contribution was as actor, designer or technician.

(10 marks)

> **Study tip** This is the body of the question. Read it carefully, your mark depends on it. You must describe what your piece was about. Remember, the examiner has no idea what you did as they did not see it, so make your description clear. You are asked to 'state' a list of aspects of your piece. If you have prepared using the advice in this chapter, you will already have a list of details you can include.

02 Explain how you developed your creative ideas for this piece of practical work. Give **at least one** specific example of how you applied your skill as actor, designer or technician in preparation for performance.

(10 marks)

> **Study tip** 'Explain' means give details. This question will always be 'an explanation of the nature of the activity undertaken by the candidate'. Here, it is the development of ideas and the application of skill that are required. Therefore, there should be a sense of development, and clear reference made to your selected skill.

03 Analyse the success of your group's ability to work as a team during the rehearsal period. You should refer to **at least one** specific example where teamwork was important in the later stages of your preparation.

(10 marks)

> **Study tip** This question will always be 'an analysis of a process'. Here, it is the analysis of teamwork in the later stages of rehearsal, with at least one example that has importance for the piece. You should be specific to **this** piece of work and consider rehearsal style activity and your own skill. Be careful: concentrating on line-learning, absences and personality clashes will not score highly.

04 Evaluate how far you achieved your personal aims in the final performance. You should refer to particular moments from the piece to support your answer.

(10 marks)

> **Study tip** This question will always be 'an evaluation of the effectiveness of the candidate's contribution'. Here, it is concerned with personal aims. If you do not mention 'aims', but instead discuss strengths and weaknesses, you will have difficulty in giving a 'clear' response and it is unlikely to be a top band answer.

Practice questions

Question 2 Choose **one** play you have studied and performed during your course. Choose **one** extract from this play. Your answer to both parts of this question should focus on acting **or** design **or** technical skills.

> **Study tip** Look at the leader carefully. Notice that it says 'studied and performed'. This is, therefore, aimed at those who have completed a controlled assessment on a scripted play. You must not answer on performances that were not taken from a scripted play.

05 Explain how you used the information provided in the original script to create your character in performance through acting skills **or** to interpret the extract through design **or** technical skills.

You may choose to refer to the stage directions from the original script and/or what characters in the text do and say.

(20 marks)

> **Study tip** To answer this question, you must explain how you used information in the script to create your character (acting) or to interpret the extract (design/technical). Actors will have learnt the script and you will be able to explain your characterisation by quoting your lines and how you performed them.

06 Analyse your personal success in presenting the extract as the playwright intended or as your group interpreted it. You should refer to particular moments from the performance and give clear reasons to support your answer.

(20 marks)

> **Study tip** This question asks for an analysis of your personal success in achieving what you set out to do. You can answer in terms of what you thought the playwright wanted, or what you and your group decided to do. 'Particular moments' are required to satisfy the demands of the question. If you consider your success in terms of moments of performance, you will score well.

Question 3 Choose one play that you have studied and worked on practically during your course. Choose **one** extract from this play. Your answer to both parts of this question should focus on your skill as designer **or** technician **or** actor.

> **Study tip** Notice that the wording of the leader is slightly different from question 2; it says 'studied and worked on practically'. Don't be thrown by this, just make sure that you concentrate on your practical work. This question, like question 2, gives you the option of design or technical or acting skills: another reason for reading both questions in the exam room before you begin to answer.

07 Explain how you developed your chosen skill in rehearsals to communicate the style, period location and/or culture selected for this extract. Give clear details of your research, rehearsal and other preparation work that you undertook.

(20 marks)

> **Study tip** This question requires you to think about the style, period, location and/or culture of the script. You do not need to include all of them but you should include at least one of them. You would score well if you considered in detail the period of the performance – with discussion of the impact on acting of wearing period costumes – or the location – with a discussion on the accent you used or aspects related to where the play takes place.

08 Analyse your success in applying what you have learnt about your chosen skill in the presentation of this extract. You should refer to particular moments from the performance and give clear reasons to support your answer.

(20 marks)

> **Study tip** This question asks you to analyse what you have learnt about your skill in undertaking this piece of work, and requires you to include 'particular moments'. Very clear responses would concentrate on moments that best demonstrated your areas of learning.

Section C: Study of a live theatre production seen

Practice questions

Question 4 Choose **one** live theatre production you have seen during your course where you saw two actors working well together in at least two scenes or sections.

Study tip First, check the leader. Read the question carefully for key words and phrases; you need to focus on 'two actors' who appeared together on stage in 'two scenes or sections'.

09 Describe in detail the skills used by these two actors in **one** scene or section from this live theatre production where they appeared together. You should include reference to the actors' voices, movement and facial expressions, and to their interaction together in this one scene or section.

(20 marks)

Study tip This question's focus on two actors means that you need to consider both adequately in terms of acting skills. You should include the actors' names as this helps you to talk about what the actors did (acting) rather than what the characters did (narrative).

10 Evaluate the success of these actors in engaging the audience through their creative co-operation in **at least one** further scene or section from this production.

(20 marks)

Study tip You need to focus here on the same two actors' performances in at least one other scene or section in terms of how well they engaged the audience. You can see that you need to have prepared to answer on more than one scene and consider the production as a whole. You should also try to make this your own personal response.

Question 5 Choose **one** live theatre production you have seen during your course where **one** area of design or technical skill was used in an inventive way.

Study tip This leader requires that the focus is on design or technical skills, and that there is a sense of inventiveness about the work you choose to write about.

11 Describe in detail what the designer or technician produced and how it was used in **at least one** scene or section to demonstrate inventiveness in your opinion.

(20 marks)

Study tip You should have engaged in some study of the play from a design or technical perspective to answer this question. You need to focus on inventiveness and how your selected aspect was used at one point in the production, so to score well you will need to select the production you use with care.

12 Evaluate the success of this design or technical skill in combining with other aspects of the performance at particular moments. Give clear reasons to support your answer.

(20 marks)

Study tip You must focus on the same area of design or technical work that you identified in 11, and then consider how well it combined with the acting or other design/technical areas. This should be at clearly identified particular moments. You must keep the question in mind at all times; it does not ask for a general discussion of as many design or technical elements that you happen to remember.

Glossary

A

Accessories: items of clothing such as hats, belts, ties or jewellery that add to the overall effect of a costume.

Angle: the direction from which the light comes onto the set.

Audience participation: directly involving the audience in the production, for example, by asking them questions or giving individuals simple tasks.

Assemble: put together items of costume that you have found to make a complete outfit.

B

Black light: use of ultraviolet lamps that cause specially treated surfaces to glow vividly when switched on; it is effective in puppetry and to give the effect of objects flying or moving by themselves on stage.

Balance: giving fair attention to other viewpoints so that the production is seen to be unbiased; this is very important when dealing with controversial topics.

Blocking: being told by the director where to stand, move or sit as you go through the first reading of the play; you can make notes of these moves in your script to help you to remember them in the next rehearsal.

C

Characterisation: the way in which an actor presents a character in a play.

Colour filter: a coloured film placed in front of a lantern to change the colour of the light on stage (also known as a gel).

Colour wheel: a disc of coloured filters that rotates to produce a rainbow effect.

Composite set: one set used throughout the production, designed to accommodate all locations and needs.

Conflict: an element of struggle, found in all drama; it may involve trying to resolve a problem or someone changing their life; it does not necessarily mean an argument.

Cross-fade: when one lighting state goes out at exactly the same time as another one comes on.

Cue sheet (lighting): a list of the lighting changes throughout the production (also known as a lighting plot).

Cue sheet (sound): a list of the sound changes throughout the production (also known as a sound plot).

Cue to cue: go through the play to all moments when there is any technical change (to lighting, sound or set) and rehearse them.

Culture: how the characters in the play live their lives.

D

Devising: planning a production and working out how it can be performed effectively.

Dimmer pack: a number of dimmer controls mounted in a cabinet.

Director: The person who tells an actor how and when to do something on stage.

Documentary: putting factual information across to the audience.

Dress rehearsal: a full rehearsal (as of a play) in costume and with stage properties shortly before the first performance.

Dynamics: the energy, speed and direction of movement you create in your performance.

E

Effects projector: a device used to project an image from a rotating glass disc to give the effect of, for example, clouds, flames or rain.

Ensemble: a group of people working together; everyone makes an equal contribution and there is no 'starring role'.

F

Flashback: when the narrative in a drama switches from the current time (current from the point of view of the characters) to an incident from the past, perhaps as a memory or a dream by one of the characters.

Flat: a light wooden frame covered in scenic canvas, plywood or hardboard which can be painted to suit your work.

Focus: concentrate the lights onto a specific area of the set.

Focus spot: light on a specific area of the stage, for example on a specific character.

Forum theatre: an interactive form of theatre developed by Brazilian director Augusto Boal; the audience stop the play to suggest different solutions to a problem that a main character is experiencing.

Fresnel: (pronounced fre-nel) the most common type of lantern used on stage, it has a textured lens and produces a very even light that is soft at the edges and tends to project a soft shadow.

G

Gauze: also known as scrim, gauze is a coarse-weave fabric which appears transparent when the scene behind it is lit; sharkstooth is the most opaque.

Gel: a coloured film placed in front of a lantern to change the colour of the light on stage.

Genre: the type of production, for example comedy, tragedy, thriller or documentary.

Get in: moving everything from storage and van onto the stage and preparing for the performance.

Get out: removing everything from the stage to storage or van.

Gobo: a small metal plate inserted behind a spotlight to project an image onto the stage.

Go cue: an instruction to the operator to carry out a change in lighting or sound.

Ground plan: a scale outline of the set drawn as if from above with indications of flats and furniture marked on it.

H

Hot-seating: the technique of an actor staying in role while answering questions from the audience about the character's thoughts and feelings; the actor can involve the audience by asking the audience for advice.

I

Illusion: anything that deceives the senses by appearing to be something which it is not.

Improvisation: a method that actors use to create, develop and communicate characters and situations so that they can make up a play. In GCSE Drama, improvisation refers to any unscripted work.

In role: appearing convincingly and consistently as a character different from one's self.

L

Lanterns: lights used to illuminate a set.

Lighting board: control desk for lighting.

Luminescent: a word that describes an item that glows in the dark when ultraviolet light is switched on.

M

Makes: items that cannot be found or borrowed and must therefore be made.

Mime: using clear gestures and movements but no words to convey a character's personality and emotions.

Monologue: when a character on stage speaks alone, sometimes directly to the audience.

Motivation: the reason why a character does something or behaves in a certain way.

Mummers' play: a traditional folk play performed usually at Christmas and involving characters such as St George.

N

Narrative: the story that your performance wants to tell the audience.

Newspanel: written messages flashing across a screen during the play, perhaps giving facts that the audience would find difficult to take in if they couldn't see them.

P

Pace: the speed and rhythm of your speech and how you pick up cues from others.

Pace-egg play: similar to a mummers' play but performed in the North of England, often on Good Friday.

Parcan: a lantern that is used to provide strong dramatic keylight, backlight or effects such as beams of light in smoke.

Patching: connecting stage lights (lanterns) to dimmer controls for fading in and out.

Period: the time period in which a play is set.

Prompt copy: a very detailed copy of the details of the performance with all cues (acting and technical) marked on it.

Prosthetics: artificial body parts; an example in stage make-up could be nose-putty, moulded to change the shape of a nose then coloured by make-up.

R

Rehearsal schedule: a list of times and places of rehearsals with the names of actors who are needed.

Rig: hang the lanterns in the correct positions.

Rostrum (plural rostra): a portable platform which you can use to create interesting levels.

S

Safe load: the maximum weight that should be put onto a lifting device or suspension point.

Scenario: the summary or outline of the plot of the play.

Setting: putting props onto a set ready for a performance and taking them off again.

Sight line: what your audience can see on the stage; sit at the extreme ends of the front row to work it out.

Society: who the characters in the play are.

Sound plot: a list of sound cues and levels in running order.

Stage form: the arrangement of the acting area and audience in your performance space.

Standby cue: a warning to the operator to be ready for a change in lighting or sound.

Status: which character is the most or least powerful in the scene; power isn't shown by shouting or towering over someone.

Stimulus (plural stimuli): the starting-point for a devised work; the idea, image or object that sparks off your work.

Striking: at the end of the performance run, the set is taken down and packed away.

Structure: organising your work, in terms of its starting point, its setting and any props that are available.

Style: how the play is performed, such as in a naturalistic fashion or physically.

Symbolic: a sign or object that represents or typifies something else; for example, a helmet and an axe might be symbolic of a fire station.

T

Target audience: the specific audience (defined, for example, by age or interest) for which a production is devised.

Tone: using your voice to express what you are feeling.

Transition: a change between scenes or sections of your work.

Index